Making NAFTA Work:
U.S. Firms and the
New North American
Business Environment

Stephen Blank and Jerry Haar

North-South Center Press
UNIVERSITY OF MIAMI

The publisher of this book is the North-South Center Press at the University of Miami.

The mission of the North-South Center is to promote better relations and serve as a catalyst for change among the United States, Canada, and the nations of Latin America and the Caribbean by advancing knowledge and understanding of the major political, social, economic, and cultural issues affecting the nations and peoples of the Western Hemisphere.

© 1998 North-South Center Press at the University of Miami.

 Published by the North-South Center Press at the University of Miami and distributed by Lynne Rienner Publishers, Inc., 1800 30th Street, Suite 314, Boulder, CO 80301-1026. All rights reserved under International and Pan-American Conventions. No portion of the contents may be reproduced or transmitted in any form, or by any means, including photocopying, recording, or any information storage retrieval system, without prior permission in writing from the North-South Center Press.

All copyright inquiries should be addressed to the publisher: North-South Center Press, 1500 Monza Avenue, Coral Gables, Florida 33146-3027, U.S.A., phone 305-284-8914, fax 305-284-5089, or e-mail mvega@nsc.msmail.miami.edu.

To order or to return books, contact Lynne Rienner Publishers, Inc., 1800 30th Street, Suite 314, Boulder, CO 80301-1026, 303-444-6684, fax 303-444-0824.

Library of Congress Cataloging-in-Publication Data

Blank, Stephen
    Making NAFTA work: U.S. firms and the new North American business environment / Stephen Blank and Jerry Haar.
        p. cm.
    Includes bibliographical references and index.
    ISBN 1-57454-047-5 (alk. paper: pbk.)
    1. Free trade—North America. 2. Free trade—United States.
    3. Investments, American—North America. I. Haar, Jerry.
II. Title.
HF1746.B58 1999   98-5602
382'.917—dc21   CIP

Printed in the United States of America/EB-NC

02 01 00 99   6 5 4 3 2

For Lenore,
Stephen

For Barbara,
Jerry

The Authors

Stephen Blank is Professor of International Business and Management and Director of the Center for International Business Development at Pace University's Lubin School of Business in New York City and Chairman of Stephen Blank Associates, an international business consulting firm. Dr. Blank's career has been involved with both business and education. In addition to his current positions at Pace University, he has taught in the Government Departments at Harvard University and the University of Pittsburgh. Among his other academic appointments are Visiting Professor of Business Administration at Dartmouth College; Adjunct Professor at Columbia University's School for International and Public Affairs; and Visiting Professor at Yale University's School of Organization and Management, the University of British Columbia, the University of Toronto, and the International University of Japan. He teaches a course each year at the École des Hautes Études Commerciales of the University of Montreal and has served as an Adjunct Senior Research Associate of the North-South Center at the University of Miami.

Jerry Haar is Senior Research Associate and Director of the Inter-American Business and Labor Program of the North-South Center at the University of Miami. He is also a Research Affiliate of the David Rockefeller Center for Latin American Studies at Harvard University and has been a Visiting Scholar at Harvard's Center for International Affairs. Dr. Haar has been an Adjunct Professor of International Business at the University of Miami's School of International Studies and Adjunct Scholar at the American Enterprise Institute in Washington, D.C. Dr. Haar was Director of Washington Programs for the Council of the Americas, a New York-based business association of over 200 companies that constitute the majority of U.S. investment in Latin America. He has held several senior staff positions with the federal government and has consulted for companies in the United States and abroad in strategic planning, risk assessment, management, marketing, and project evaluation.

Table of Contents

Preface

Four years after its inception, the North American Free Trade Agreement (NAFTA) remains controversial. For many U.S. citizens, the agreement has become a repository of frustrations regarding an array of issues that affect our lives, including globalization, free trade, economic dislocation, job insecurity, ethnic paranoia, and the future of the American middle class. NAFTA has become a lightning rod for widespread and deeply felt fears about economic life in the twenty-first century, and the debate over its extension to Chile and perhaps to the rest of the Western Hemisphere has drawn the concerned attention of politicians, labor and business leaders, environmentalists, specialists in social policy, and journalists.[1]

Remarkable charges have been laid against NAFTA. In one recently released report, opponents of the agreement contend that NAFTA has put downward pressure on American wages and living standards, created deep and probably chronic trade deficits with Canada and Mexico, displaced more than 400,000 jobs, weakened workers' rights, reduced employee bargaining power, exacerbated environmental and public-health damage along the U.S.-Mexico border, compromised food safety standards, and increased drug trafficking due to insufficient border inspections and heavier truck traffic from Mexico.[2] "NAFTA is the trade agreement from hell," states Lori Wallach, director of Public Citizens Global Trade Watch, "The United States has gotten clobbered."[3]

Many deny these catastrophic criticisms. One analyst argues that if we use the U.S. Commerce Department's estimate that every $1 billion increase in exports translates into 22,800 new jobs, then 55 percent of the 8.8 million jobs created between 1993 and 1996 were due to export growth. Since exports to Mexico and Canada grew by 10 percent in this period, it is reasonable to claim that almost 10 percent of these jobs could be accounted for by NAFTA-related exports.[4] U.S. Trade Representative Charlene Barshefsky says that exports to Canada and Mexico support 2.3 million U.S. jobs, up from 1.9 million before NAFTA came into effect.[5] Others claim that imports have had a relatively minor impact on the decline of the share of U.S. workers employed in manufacturing. Technology advancements and the changing composition of domestic spending are more powerful causes of changes in the demand for labor.[6] There just has not been enough time, say other experts, to know whether labor and environmental conditions in Mexico have deteriorated since NAFTA, improved significantly, or remained the same, particularly given Mexico's adverse economic circumstances since December 1994.

The U.S. government, in its own evaluation of NAFTA after three years, argues that trade in North America has increased remarkably, that trade barriers — particularly Mexican — have fallen substantially, and that NAFTA has contributed to America's economic expansion. NAFTA, President Bill Clinton's report contends, has had "a modest positive effect" on income, investment, and jobs supported by exports.[7] Some experts feel that NAFTA's real value was illustrated by Mexico's decision not to apply import restrictions during the peso crisis of December 1994 but to maintain its commitment to trade liberalization, even under such difficult circumstances.[8]

One result of this controversy is that the expansion of NAFTA remains in serious doubt. The 1997 failure to secure fast-track negotiating authority from Congress has resulted in more than a broken promise to Chile. It has jeopardized the larger process of hemispheric economic integration, by which NAFTA would be transformed into a Free Trade Area of the Americas (FTAA), including all countries in the Western Hemisphere. As U.S. leadership has waned, MERCOSUR, the Southern Cone Common Market, continues to gain momentum.

Our view is that this focus on NAFTA itself misses the point about what is happening today in North America's economy. The real story, we believe, is deepening economic integration in North America and the emergence of a true North American economy. This process did not begin with NAFTA or the Canada-U.S. Free Trade Agreement (CUSFTA); trade liberalization and the emergence of new cross-border business strategies preceded NAFTA. Indeed, both of these agreements can best be viewed as responses to deep, underlying change already underway in the structure of our economies.[9] This profound change in patterns, structures, and strategies of business around the world, and especially in North America, is being driven by the interlinked forces of global competition, regulatory liberalization, and technology.

The aim of our research has been to gain a better understanding of how managers in major U.S. companies view changes underway in the North American economy and of how their firms are responding to this new environment. We seek to identify key drivers, explore changes in corporate structure and strategy, and suggest trends that might be expected to take shape in the future.

This study, undertaken by the North-South Center, builds on two earlier investigations. One was carried out by The Conference Board of Canada in 1992 and the second by the Americas Society in 1995.

The authors are most grateful to the North-South Center, University of Miami, and its Director Ambler H. Moss, Jr., and Deputy Director Robin L. Rosenberg for their financial support of the Mexican phase of the project and to Harvard University's Center of International Affairs and the David Rockefeller Center for Latin American Studies and their respective Directors, Jorge Domínguez and John H. Coatsworth, for valuable academic support.

We thank the National Planning Association for permitting us to make use of materials published in the *North American Outlook*, research that was supported financially by the Americas Society and the Royal Bank of Canada and carried out by Stephen Blank, Stephen Krajewski, and Henry Yu.

Invaluable research assistance was also provided by North-South Center Fellows Ana Lorena Tamargo, Manuel Mindreau, Françoise Marco, and Diane DeWindt, as well as librarian Rebecca Smith of the Harvard Business School. The North-South Center's Norma Laird and Nancy Colón typed the manuscript. The North-South Center Press's Kathleen Hamman edited, Mary D'León copy edited and proofread, and Mary Mapes formatted the text and designed the cover.

Stephen Blank
Jerry Haar

Chapter One

Introduction and Methodology

This book represents the third in a series of linked studies that examine the impact of the changing environment of business in North America on corporate strategy and structure. The first study was carried out by the Conference Board of Canada in 1991-1992, in the first years after the Canada-U.S. Free Trade Agreement (CUSFTA). Stephen Krajewski was the primary researcher. This study examined the impact of CUSFTA on the Canadian subsidiaries of U.S. firms, relying in large measure on a survey of managers in these Canadian operations. The Conference Board report, entitled *Multinational Firms Across the Canada-U.S. Border: An Investigation of Intrafirm Trade and Other Activities*, was published early in 1992.[10] Throughout this book, we refer to the first study as "the Canadian study" or "the Conference Board of Canada study."

A second study was undertaken in 1994 against the background of the recent passage of the North American Free Trade Agreement (NAFTA). Research was carried out by Stephen Blank and Stephen Krajewski, with the assistance of Henry Yu, and supported financially by the Royal Bank of Canada and the Americas Society in New York. A report based on this investigation, *U.S. Firms in North America: Redefining Structure and Strategy,* was published in 1995 in a monograph series sponsored by the National Planning Association.[11] This second study, for which a survey of U.S. companies also was conducted, sought to test and enlarge the Conference Board of Canada study and incorporated findings (as well as unpublished data) from the first study's survey.

The relationship between these first two studies was largely fortuitous. For the second study, Stephen Krajewski was able to join Stephen Blank at the Americas Society in a project that had recently been funded by the Royal Bank of Canada. With the generous assistance of the Conference Board of Canada, Krajewski brought additional unpublished materials drawn from his Canadian research into the new project. Blank and Krajewski sought to extend the Conference Board of Canada's research and findings, but the new project was focused more directly on corporate structure and strategy. Questionnaires were directed to U.S. corporate headquarters executives with key responsibilities for strategic management, instead of the firms' Canadian subsidiaries. Targets were senior managers with interests and backgrounds in corporate organization and strategy rather than those with specific responsibilities for Canadian or Mexican operations. Throughout this book, for the sake of brevity, the second study is referred to as "the Americas Society study"; however, it should be noted that without the Royal Bank of Canada, the Conference Board of Canada, and the Washington, D.C.-based National Planning Association, the research and its publication would not have been possible.

The relationship between the second and third studies was more carefully planned. The third questionnaire survey was carried out in 1994 by Jerry Haar of the

North-South Center at the University of Miami, with extensive follow-up queries in 1995 and 1996, following the peso devaluation of December 20, 1994. The survey instrument used in this third phase of the project replicated with only minor changes the second study's questionnaire. Polled in 1994, 1995, and 1996 for the third phase were senior managers of U.S. corporate operations in Mexico, providing us with a third data set. The first data set was managers of U.S. subsidiaries in Canada (the Canadian study, 1992); the second, managers of U.S. firms at corporate headquarters (the Americas Society study, 1995); and third, managers of U.S. subsidiaries in Mexico (the North-South Center study, 1994-1996).

As the present book seeks to build on all of the earlier research, it integrates the responses from the North-South Center's third survey in Mexico with the Americas Society report published by the National Planning Association and also draws upon the findings of the Conference Board of Canada survey. Additionally, it contains historical, economic, and political analysis, particularly of Mexico.

Two caveats with regard to this research should be noted at the start. First, we emphasize that none of the three surveys involved large samples. Thirty-four firms completed a confidential questionnaire in the second study, 37 in the third. (A total of 52 companies participated in the second and third phases of the project. They are listed in the Appendix.) Survey data were supported in both cases by face-to-face and telephone interviews and by extensive documentary research, but our findings should be viewed as indicative of trends and patterns rather than statistically conclusive.

Second, the focus of this research is largely on companies involved in manufacturing where, clearly, the emergence of cross-border networks has been most intense, advanced, and, by and large, consistent. In the service sector, there is more variety, and in certain sectors there remain more inhibitions to North American (or even U.S.-Canadian) integration.

Key Findings

Three key findings are apparent. First, even before NAFTA was ratified, an emerging North American regional market had become a centerpoint of many firms' strategic outlooks. A senior vice president of international operations at a major paper and packaging firm echoed other respondents when he stated, "Business is so far ahead of politicians on this one that it almost makes the agreement secondary. To many in our industry, NAFTA is a fait accompli."[12]

U.S. firms are adapting their corporate strategies and structures to an evolving North American economic architecture. In so doing, their efforts to respond to this new situation further accelerate the emergence of a North American economic system. The result is a reinforcing cycle of change that is eroding national borders beyond the capacity of governments to control.

Second, our research suggests strongly that changes in North American corporate organization and strategy have been more rapid than anyone anticipated. Cross-border corporate integration has been deeper and more far-reaching, we believe, than governments in particular seem to realize.

Third, our investigation supports the view that direct investment is far less volatile than portfolio investment. For example, unlike the owners of "hot money," who fled from the Mexican market when the peso was devalued in December 1994, most multinational firms' responses were based upon long-term fundamentals. Variables such as factor endowments; production efficiency; geographic and technological competitiveness; size, growth, and demographic characteristics of the internal consumer market; and location advantage (such as exportability) together carry more weight than issues such as economic nationalism in Canada and exchange rate instability in Mexico.

Respondents in these surveys identified NAFTA with the emergence of a continental economy rather than more narrowly with the legal accord itself. However, the driving force behind change in strategy and structure was not solely the CUSFTA or NAFTA, even in this broader definition. Change was being driven by a much broader array of forces, including the recession of the early 1990s, continued slow growth, intensified global competition, changes in technology, and the rapidly shifting perceptions of senior executives in major firms.

The emergence of a new North American economic architecture both reflects and affects wider trends in the global economy. What is happening in North America is a dimension of the global transformation in the relations between states and markets, between governments and firms, and among economic, financial, trade, and investment systems. Deepening corporate integration in North America is, as well, one of a wide array of changes in corporate strategy, structure, and operations over the past 15 years. Efforts to create and sustain superior performance, install total quality, enhance service, manage across borders, maximize productivity, apply innovative technologies, and reengineer and reduce costs have significantly transformed the competitive environment of global business.

Multiple, powerful, and complex pressures are reshaping corporations and their operations. Changes are taking place in corporate organization and strategy of a magnitude that is comparable only to the restructuring of corporate organization that occurred at the end of the nineteenth century. We look here at one dimension of a much wider set of events. Our investigation shows clearly the extent of strategic and structural change underway in a sample of key U.S. firms. For most, we will see that the three countries of North America are increasingly viewed as a single, regional economic "space," a rapidly emerging North American economy.

Our discussions with executives in these firms and the case studies we have undertaken strongly suggest that this new focus on North America was not typically the result of a long, gradual, well-thought-out evolution. It was not the culmination of a slowly dawning awareness of an emerging North American economic system. More frequently, we think, these firms confronted a drastically changing and threatening world at the end of the 1980s. Many responded by launching a wide range of initiatives — some complementary, some competitive. Some slimmed down, closed plants, and laid off workers and managers; some expanded. They put new management systems in place and brought new technologies on line. They reorganized and restructured, globalized and localized. And, as part of all of this, they lurched toward new North American structures as well.

If we turn our vision to the future, will we see these trends and patterns strengthening or changing once again? Will this new North American focus be firmly institutionalized in corporate strategies and structures? Cross-border networks have surely become more pervasive and intensive in North America. But the focus on North America may be diminishing. Regionalization in the "Triad" as the primary organizing principle for international business — the view of the early 1990s — was rivaled in the past few years by burgeoning enthusiasm for the big emerging markets (BEMs), including, of course, China.

In addition, and perhaps more critically, the growing impact of technology may be altering the rules of the whole game. As companies outsource more activities and as traditionally integrated companies become more like those James Brian Quinn calls "intellectual holding companies,"[13] North America may diminish in importance as a strategic concept. Information technology is rapidly reducing transaction costs and enabling independent companies to collaborate in ways not even conceivable a few years ago. The result is that volatility in corporate organization has not declined, and companies have continued in the past few years to swing from one organizational format to another.

Nonetheless, for many firms in many industries, in manufacturing and in services as well, the borders between Canada and the United States and, to a somewhat lesser extent, between the United States and Mexico are vanishing. If one looks back 20 years to the mid-1970s, the differences in the structure of North America's economy are overwhelming. Many manufacturing firms have put highly integrated continental strategies in place. The energy and transportation industries are more firmly integrated across North America than anyone could possibly have anticipated only a short while ago. As Brent Jang stated, "The Canadian oil patch has formed a bold economic alliance with the United States, reducing energy links within Canada and preparing to export record amounts of crude oil to thirsty U.S. markets." In the same article, Raymond Chrétien, Canadian ambassador to the United States, observed, "There will be winners on all fronts. Canada is very much accepted as part of a North American oil and gas market."[14] Despite continued irritations on both sides of the border — for example, regarding softwood lumber, salmon, and magazine advertising — Canadians and Americans live increasingly in a single economy.

It is within this dynamic, rapidly changing milieu that we embarked upon our research, in an effort to gauge and document how U.S. multinational companies are responding to the new economic and business environment taking shape in North America.

Chapter Two

U.S. Foreign Investment in Canada and Mexico

The emergence of an integrated North American economy dates not from the signing of the North American Free Trade Agreement in 1993, but from 1982, when the collapse of oil prices made it clear that Canadian and Mexican import-substitution development strategies were no longer tenable. From that moment onward to the creation of the CUSFTA and NAFTA, the issue was not whether a North American economic system would emerge but exactly what type of arrangement would be made.

U.S. Direct Investment in Canada

Canadian attitudes toward foreign investment in the past 20 years have been deeply ambivalent. Foreign direct investment (FDI), while welcomed for the economic benefits it brings, has been widely perceived as a significant constraint on Canada's national autonomy and sovereignty and a threat to its cultural identity. Therefore, CUSFTA and NAFTA symbolize a major shift in Canada's trade and investment policies, from import substitution to regional outwardness.

Unlike the United States, where economic development in large measure has preceded government, Canada's economy was very much a creation *of* government. The term "defensive expansionism" is used to describe the role played by the Canadian state in building a national infrastructure to defend Canada's political autonomy and economic independence vis-à-vis the United States, particularly in the years following Confederation in 1867.

From the late 1800s through the years following World War II, Canada's national industrial strategy was based on a policy of import substitution within the British Empire and Commonwealth. Prime Minister John A. Macdonald's National Policy was an explicit attempt by Canadian governments in the late nineteenth century to enhance the economic and political integration of Canada by constructing a national railway system to link the country from East to West, by encouraging immigration and the growth of agriculture to open Canada's West, and by stimulating industrial development with a high tariff to discourage imports and encourage foreign investment. Canada's independence would be guaranteed by a national economy strong enough to offset the North-South attraction of its enormous neighbor.

The National Policy protected secondary industry and forced foreign firms to invest in manufacturing operations. Canada encouraged inward flows of foreign capital with an openness to foreign investment rare in the modern world.[15] The exploitation and worldwide marketing of Canada's natural resources financed an

5

import-substitution manufacturing industry (Canada's "branch plant" economy) and high levels of social expenditure.

Freer trade and closer economic integration with the United States have been recurring issues throughout Canadian history. A reciprocal trade agreement in 1854 was abrogated by the United States during the Civil War, and bilateral free trade arrangements were discussed during the 1870s, in 1911, and again in 1948. In 1965, the Auto Pact rationalized the automobile industry on a bilateral basis.

U.S. investment in Canada increased rapidly after 1945 with enthusiastic Canadian approval. By the late 1960s, however, most Canadians had come to feel that there was enough U.S. involvement in their economy, and many believed too many U.S. multinational corporations were operating in Canada.[16] Canadians were increasingly determined to diversify their economy and increase the weight of manufacturing, particularly Canadian-owned industry. A growing number of Canadians feared that rising levels of foreign investment were weakening Canadian control over key areas of national life. Kari Levitt and other economic nationalists argued that Canada's economic development benefited foreign owners of capital more than Canadians, and that these investments perpetuated Canada's status as a hewer of wood and drawer of water vis-à-vis other countries and in particular the United States. In Levitt's view, Canada was "the world's richest underdeveloped country."[17]

Canadian public policy in the 1970s responded to these concerns. Efforts were undertaken by Ottawa to alter the competitive status in favor of Canadian-owned firms or, more frequently, to give special attention to Canadian-owned firms. At the same time, the Canadian government tried to pressure foreign-owned firms to adjust their behavior to conform more to Canadian interests (although the precise definition of "Canadian interests" remained uncertain and controversial).

In the early 1970s, Canada seemed to confront three options for the future. It could maintain the present situation with the United States, encourage a still closer relationship with the United States or, as a "third option," seek to diversify its involvements on a global basis and reduce its vulnerability to the United States.

Although many political leaders favored it, the third option was no option at all. Despite efforts to diversify Canada's economic linkages, bilateral economic integration increased rapidly. In 1954, Canada sent 33 percent of its exports to and received 13 percent of its imports from the United Kingdom and other Western European nations. But in 1984, these markets accounted for only 6 percent of Canadian exports and 9 percent of its imports. By this time, approximately 80 percent of Canada's expanding trade was carried on with the United States in what had become the world's largest bilateral trade relationship.

Strenuous efforts were made during these years to reshape the relationship between U.S. firms and their Canadian subsidiaries. In 1972, the most comprehensive of a series of reports on the impact of foreign investment was published. *Foreign Direct Investment in Canada* (the "Gray Report") summarized earlier studies and advanced a series of new arguments. The report underscored the possible imbalance between the manufacturing and resource sectors that might be created or exacerbated by multinational corporate activity. It stressed, too, the tendency of U.S. subsidiaries in Canada to replicate the full range of products produced by the parent firm, at significantly higher cost levels in the smaller Canadian market.

Closely identified with the Gray Report was the notion of the "truncated" firm as the malign result of development driven by foreign investment. The truncated firm is a branch plant that fails to perform all of the essential tasks associated with the development, production, and marketing activities of a "normal" firm: "The truncated subsidiary is one in which key functions are absent, being in the hands of the parent organization. The deficiencies most often mentioned are top management, research and development, and exports."[18]

These concerns led the Canadian government to increase pressure on foreign parent companies and potential investors to provide greater benefits to Canada. Such benefits included expanded Canadian equity participation, more Canadian members on subsidiary boards, enhanced local research and development, and expanded exports. Critics of foreign investment and Canadian managers in multinational firms alike demanded that Canadian operations be granted "world product mandates," giving the subsidiary full responsibility for a product from initial research through development, production, and international marketing. A new government organization, the Foreign Investment Review Agency (FIRA), was created to serve as a vehicle for negotiating better deals for Canada with foreign investors.[19]

Branch plants, it was argued, failed to provide sufficient opportunity for Canadian managers. Canadian managers had little freedom in decisionmaking, and their career development was stunted in key areas of research and development, export, and investment. Subsidiaries were strongly encouraged to wrest greater autonomy from corporate headquarters. Often, the most passionate demands for change came from Canadian managers in the subsidiary. "Good Canadian managers," one Canadian executive in a U.S. firm said, in an interview in 1975, "will fight for more autonomy."[20]

Some Canadian executives proposed that multinational corporations adopt a more decentralized structure. The former CEO of General Electric's Canadian subsidiary suggested a "commonwealth" system be put in place — a highly decentralized organization in which basic business strategies would be set by subsidiary managers rather than by corporate headquarters. "The commonwealth relationship," he wrote, "lets the subsidiary attain a high level of autonomy with innovative design, production and marketing capability." The subsidiary in this model actually might seek opportunities involving "risk ventures to meet national needs that are competitive with undertakings in which the parent is engaged."[21]

Although some fought against the trend, most U.S. firms responded by trying to be good "corporate citizens" in Canada. Boards, equity, and management were all "Canadianized" to some degree, and Canadian subsidiaries of many U.S. firms won greater autonomy. Disagreement focused not so much on the goal of greater local autonomy and heightened benefits for Canada, which most headquarters and subsidiary managers appeared to accept, but rather on the means to achieve these goals, whether through voluntary arrangements or by government regulation.

The oil price rises of 1973 and 1979 seemed God-given gifts to Canada. In Prime Minister Pierre Trudeau's view, windfall profits gained from oil price increases would enable Canada to reconstruct its foreign-owned manufacturing-based economy into a new, "Made in Canada," post-industrial economy. But the oil was owned by the provinces, and Canadians found themselves with not one but 11 competing industrial strategies. Moreover, the companies that found, extracted, and marketed the oil were almost all U.S. owned and wary, to say the least, of these new ideas. Ten years of complex turmoil unfolded — between Ottawa and the provinces (or, perhaps more accurately, between Central Canada and the energy rich provinces) and between Canada and the United States. Tension with foreign firms mounted in these years as Ottawa tried to use rising oil prices to intensify pressure for greater Canadian autonomy and increased Canadian benefits. The National Energy Policy brought these struggles to a head, with some U.S. firms complaining bitterly about expropriation.

The collapse of world oil prices in 1982 was devastating to the Canadian government, deeply embroiled in conflicts with the provinces, experiencing the worst relations with the U.S. government in memory, and confronting a gaping budgetary deficit. The 1982 crisis led to a remarkable U-turn in Canadian policy, as a chastened Liberal government sought to open discussions with Washington on plans for a sectoral free trade accord. Brian Mulroney's Progressive Conservative party won a tremendous victory in the 1984 general election, and, although Mulroney had opposed a free trade agreement with the United States during the election campaign, he soon turned his attention as Prime Minister to the CUSFTA negotiations, which were concluded early in 1989.

The general election of 1988 was fought essentially as a referendum on the Canada-U.S. Free Trade Agreement, and the number of Canadians who voted for parties that opposed CUSFTA was greater than those who voted for the Tories who favored it. Over the next few years, however, the influence of Canadian economic nationalists declined dramatically. The election of 1994 virtually eliminated the New Democratic Party from Parliament and shifted the spectrum of representation to parties that viewed foreign investment more favorably.

Canadian attitudes toward foreign investment remained ambivalent even after the creation of CUSFTA. Free trade has been a lightning rod, drawing the blame for almost every economic and political malaise. As one leading opponent of CUSFTA contended, "The free trade agreement . . . challenges every single part of this distinct Canadian system and, in so doing, threatens the very survival of our country."[22]

When Mexican President Carlos Salinas de Gortari and U.S. President George Bush announced that talks would begin on a comprehensive bilateral trade agreement, Canadian leaders were forced to respond. The CUSFTA had come into effect in January 1989, and there were few obvious reasons for Canada to enter another round of negotiations including Mexico, "especially with a country with which there were few trade and investment ties, that had a much lower standard of living and level of wages, and that was a clear competitor for the U.S. market."[23]

In the late summer and fall of 1990, the Canadian government conducted public hearings on whether Canada should participate in negotiations on a possible NAFTA. But in September, before the hearings were completed, Minister of International Trade John Crosbie announced that Canada would seek to enter negotiations with the United States and Mexico. The three countries announced on February 1, 1991, that negotiations on a North American free trade agreement would begin.

At that time, trade and investment ties between Canada and Mexico were small. In 1989, Mexican exports to Canada totaled C$1.68 billion and Canadian exports to Mexico, C$1 billion.[24] Canada was Mexico's eleventh largest trading partner, and Mexico was Canada's seventeenth largest trading partner, less important to Canada than South Korea, Taiwan, France, or Italy. Nearly three-quarters of Canadian trade was with the United States, whereas Latin America and the Caribbean (LAC) accounted for less than 5 percent — and only one-third of that was with Mexico.

Canadian private foreign investment in Latin America as a whole was not insignificant, amounting to $8 billion in 1989. In that year, the stock of Canadian investment in LAC exceeded Canadian investment in Europe outside the United Kingdom, although Canadian investment in the United Kingdom was greater than Canadian-held investment in LAC. However, Canadian investment in Mexico was only about $400 million, and there was no significant Mexican investment in Canada.

From the Canadian perspective, there were both positive and negative reasons to participate in the NAFTA project, although the negative reasons were probably more important. The hope that existing low levels of trade and investment with Mexico might be increased was one incentive for a free trade arrangement. Another was the need to rationalize North American industry on a continental basis and to make the region stronger in the face of increased global competition. In 1991, Leonard Waverman observed that a free trade agreement would also provide significant political advantages to Mexico and Canada because together they could offset protectionist measures in the United States. The United States would not be able to play one country against the other.[25]

Negative reasons outweighed the positive, however, in getting Canada to the NAFTA negotiating table. Of particular importance was the need to ensure that Canada offered investors (of any country) the same advantage of free access to all three markets as did the United States. If Washington negotiated a series of bilateral free trade agreements with other countries of the region, a "hub and spoke" trading system could emerge in which the United States, as the "hub," would have a locational advantage over any of the "spokes."[26] Another important reason to negotiate a NAFTA was to protect Canada's recently acquired interests in the U.S. market by being involved in any negotiations touching the auto sector, rules of origin, and the phasing-in of liberalization measures. Several studies, in addition, underlined the risks of some trade diversion away from Canada due to the possible overlap between Mexican and Canadian products.

In the course of the negotiations, Canadians began to recognize what was happening in Mexico. More Canadian firms were exploring business opportunities in Mexico. The Canadian Embassy in Mexico City reported that more than 4,500 potential Canadian exporters visited the embassy in 1992,[27] and the Quebec government launched its own campaign to promote NAFTA. Canadian firms increasingly were coming to see Mexico as an opportunity, even while many labor groups continued to see NAFTA as a threat.

There was a growing hope, too, that the new trade deal with Mexico would lead to greater economic involvement for Canada with the rest of Latin America. Influential Canadians predicted that as the impact of the debt crisis in Latin America subsided and growth resumed, imports would increase substantially. Liberalized trade in the Western Hemisphere might then provide important advantages for Canada. It also became clearer that NAFTA offered significant improvements over CUSFTA.[28]

Finally, the Canadian government was determined to protect the gains it had won in the free trade agreement with the United States. As one observer noted, "For Canada, the negotiations are basically about how to include Mexico in the North American economy, not an opportunity to re-open the FTA or deal with the 'unfinished American agenda.' Canada's basic position is defensive — to protect the FTA."[29]

The Changing Treatment of Foreign Investment in Mexico

The course of FDI in Mexico has been shaped by the forces of nationalism, political and economic development, and changes in both the regional and global economies. Late twentieth-century industrialization and the twin currents of multinational corporate competition and regional economic integration are shaping patterns of foreign investment and the responses of host country governments.

FDI in Mexico, while never a large share of total investment (about 10 percent of total gross fixed investment in the 1980s), has been significant in Mexico's economic growth.[30] In 1996, FDI in Mexico reached US$63.8 billion.

Historical Background

At the start of the Mexican Revolution in 1910, U.S. investment in Mexico represented approximately 38 percent of total foreign capital. Proportionately, this was greater than the volume of European capital inflows to the United States during its most intensive period of economic development.[31] In 1996, the United States accounted for 63 percent of Mexico's FDI. Initially, the dominant presence of U.S. investors in Mexico was confined to infrastructure and natural resources. During the government of Gen. Porfirio Díaz, who ruled from 1877 until 1910 (the *Porfiriato*), a significant transformation of Mexico's economy began, and U.S. capital flowed in, followed by European.[32]

Regional tariffs were abolished for almost 35 years during the Porfiriato, although national tariffs for all but capital and intermediate goods were raised. Infrastructure, especially railroads, was expanded, minerals and other raw materials were developed, and private initiatives were fostered.[33] Mexico's gross domestic product (GDP) more than tripled in real terms during the Porfiriato, and foreign trade as a share of GDP increased by more than 10 percentage points.[34] Nevertheless, a small internal market, lack of a modern banking system, and high levels of market concentration meant that only oligopolies could survive. Additionally, the absence of a well-developed banking infrastructure required the merchant elite to finance business through the reinvestment of accumulated profits.

As for the government assuming an activist role in national development, this was not to be the case. Public investment never accounted for more than 5 percent of total investment, and public expenditures for capital formation never exceeded 7 percent. Income inequality and growth disparities also widened. Clearly, the Porfiriato's "primary contradiction" was in its results: the growing imbalance between rapid economic growth and the slow pace of political and social progress.[35] This scenario served as a prelude to the Mexican Revolution of 1910.

The role of the state in the economy expanded as a result of the revolution — a role that was linked to the ideological and political grounding of the revolution itself, particularly as it regarded the social function of private property.[36] Mexico remained open to foreign capital, but the state played a more prominent role. During the 1930s and 1940s, import-substitution industrialization (ISI) began. With the nationalization of oil and other *dirigiste* actions, the interventionist administration of Lázaro Cárdenas (1934-1940) set the course for a relationship between labor and capital in which the state functioned as the mediator — the "proper" role being to mediate in favor of the weaker party, namely labor.[37] Regulation of foreign investment continued at a slower pace until the 1970s, when the Law for the Promotion of Mexican Investment (1973) was passed, strictly limiting the areas in which foreign equity was allowed and instituting 51-percent Mexican ownership as a general rule for new foreign investments. The law created the National Commission on Foreign Investment (NCFI) to regulate FDI. A second law created the Registry on Technology Transfer to review all new foreign contracts. However, 100 percent foreign ownership was permitted in the automotive industry, providing that companies incorporated local suppliers or met export-performance requirements.[38]

The Mexican Economy in the 1980s

Paralleling the Canadian experience in the mid-1980s, Mexico's attitude toward FDI changed radically from a cautious, nationalist, defensive stance to a more open internationalist one, with a strong commitment to integrate Mexico into the global economy.[39]

The first half of the 1980s was a period of turmoil for Mexico, as both external and internal crises — oil, debt, interest rates, and capital flight — wracked the economy. Between 1979 and 1981, the most critical shock to Mexico was caused by capital flight, which amounted to nearly $10 billion in 1981 alone. In 1982, when the oil rush came to an end and Mexico's debt crisis reached its highest point, José López-Portillo's administration (1976-1982) reacted by nationalizing the domestic banking system, thus generating new outward flows of capital. Mexico had been able to increase its debt easily, given its large oil reserves. The 1978-1980 subsidies, incentives, and transfers undertaken by the public sector outstripped the government's income stream; external indebtedness increased at record levels for both the public and private sectors.

As in Canada, the major change in Mexico took place in 1982, though much more profoundly. Miguel de la Madrid (1982-1988) came to office with a whole new economic program: to decrease government expenditures, impose wage and price controls, and renegotiate with foreign creditors.[40] However, renegotiating the debt on terms that reduced both interest payments and the principal (through provisions for debt-to-equity swaps and debt capitalization) and raising domestic interest rates did not produce the expected results. A new approach to foreign investment was adopted in 1984, based on a sectorally targeted strategy; accordingly, regulations were eased in exchange for concessions by foreign firms. Furthermore, the 1985 law that introduced the System of Coordination of Commitments and Goals made authorization for foreign companies easier by requiring only the approval of the NCFI. De la Madrid imposed an economic liberalization strategy, including a broad commitment to privatization.

This shift in policy meant abandoning Mexico's import-substitution policy that had precluded the free trade of foreign goods into Mexico.[41] In 1986, Mexico joined the General Agreement on Tariffs and Trade (GATT), further opening its markets to foreign industrial and consumer goods and reducing its trade barriers from 100 percent to 20 percent.[42] After joining GATT, Mexico eliminated most export permits and reduced export taxes and direct export subsidies. To slow down inflation and make Mexican exports more competitive in foreign markets, the peso was devalued against the U.S. dollar by approximately 432 percent between 1985 and 1988.[43]

Carlos Salinas de Gortari, Mexico's president from 1988 through 1994, continued and expanded the liberalization of the economy, including a privatization program marked by the sale of the national telephone company, Telmex, and the national airline, Aeroméxico.[44] In May 1989, the government further liberalized foreign investment in Mexico to permit foreign investors to hold up to 100 percent equity of new investments in unclassified areas if they met some specific requirements.[45] Subsequently, more than 25 areas of the economy were deregulated, with private and foreign participation permitted in sectors such as petrochemicals, trucking, telecommunications, financial services, and food distribution. The banking sector was reprivatized through a constitutional amendment, although foreign majority ownership was still not permitted.

Mexico's 1989 Foreign Investment Law was a major step in the direction of market opening policies and liberalized investment rules.[46] Although industrial promotion in Mexico has been cautious toward and restrictive of FDI, there has been ample evidence during the last 20 years of its great potential in a complementary role.[47] Evidence shows that 1) productivity levels of locally owned firms have converged with those of foreign owned firms; 2) the rate of productivity growth of local firms relates positively to the degree of foreign ownership of an industry; 3) the productivity gap between Mexican and U.S. firms between the mid-1960s and mid-1980s has diminished; and 4) the rate of productivity growth of Mexican industries and Mexico's rate of convergence with the United States are higher in industries with a greater presence of FDI.

Foreign firms' contributions to technical progress in Mexican industry have mainly been in the installation of internationally competitive production capacity and the establishment of a supply network. Foreign firms have financed the development of technology in research centers and academic institutions, and foreign firms have underwritten almost 50 percent of the funding for research and development in the country.[48] Increasingly, global production across industries and product lines will be accompanied by the spread of opportunities in secondary firms servicing the industry leaders.

The Salinas government also embarked upon the task of joining Mexico's future to that of its northern neighbors by proposing a free trade agreement with the United States. Salinas opened negotiations with the Bush administration in June 1990 and agreed to a progressive changeover to free trade in goods and services.[49] On September 25, 1990, President Bush notified Congress of the intentions of both countries to enter fast-track negotiations for an FTA with Mexico. Later, Canada announced its support for NAFTA, which eventually led to a joint communiqué issued on February 5, 1991, announcing a trilateral agreement, separate from CUSFTA.[50]

Speeding the Reforms: Continued Efforts to Liberalize Mexico's Economy

The origins of Mexico's drive toward a more open economy lay in the mid-1980s, when its inability to pay the external debt had convinced many businesspeople in the Mexican private sector that the old import-substitution strategy — which implied protection from foreign competition and barriers to free trade — was exhausted and that new directions had to be pursued.[51] Support for NAFTA originated in Mexico's private sector, as firms developed new strategies to mitigate the effects of the economic recession, and was only later backed officially by the Salinas administration.

Mexico has been making a concerted effort to speed the reforms contained in NAFTA, which went into effect on January 1, 1994, in many cases enacting them faster than required. These include the expansion of equity investments to non-stock-market companies and the sectoral openings in transport, communications, and real estate. To encourage the continued flow of foreign funds, Mexico enacted a new Foreign Investment Law, which took effect on December 28, 1993. The law extends to all foreign investors many of the rights held by U.S. and Canadian firms under NAFTA, which receive the same treatment as national firms in Mexico, and opens almost all of the sectors to the North Americans. With this legislation, Mexico has built on the liberalization initiated in 1989 by eliminating the main restrictive criteria (that an investment must be less than $100 million and be located outside certain metropolitan areas) to qualify for automatic approval in nonregulated sectors.[52]

Restrictions on foreign participation in regulated sectors have been compiled into one law instead of being scattered in different decrees. Oil, electricity, postal service, and railways remain reserved for the state, and television and radio broadcasting are reserved for Mexicans. Other regulated sectors are airlines and cable TV, where foreigners are limited to minority holdings, and cellular telephone service and oil and gas pipelines, where approval is needed for majority foreign ownership. Previous restrictions on land ownership within certain border and seacoast areas have been lifted for business and industrial purposes.[53] Whether an investment is indirect or portfolio, any neutral investment, by which an investor has all the rights of a shareholder except the right to vote, is no longer restricted to companies trading on the Mexican stock market. The law also provides for future elimination of restrictions on foreign investment in the autoparts industry and transportation.

This less restrictive regulatory environment, coupled with NAFTA and strong markets, increased activity in new plant openings, joint ventures, and mergers and acquisitions (M&A) involving foreign companies. Although traditionally the most dynamic sectors have been industrial, such as automotive, petrochemicals, electronics, metals, and food processing, the services sector received a growing amount of foreign investment as well.

Local content requirements also have been de-emphasized. Now that NAFTA is in effect, there has been more focus on North American content, with preferential tariff treatment granted to goods that satisfy the rules of origin outlined in the agreement. A 1990 decree still requires 36-percent local content for automobiles, but under NAFTA this will gradually be eliminated. For U.S. and Canadian firms, NAFTA has also liberalized the local content requirements for large public sector contracts.

Mexican trade is governed by the Foreign Trade Law of 1993 and the customs law, revised the same year. The Foreign Trade Law created the Foreign Trade Commission (the federal agency responsible for regulating foreign trade), which brings dumping and subsidized production into the definition of unfair trade practices and details the procedure for imposing countervailing duties. Tariffs, import licenses, and quotas are allowed as safeguard measures, but only on a temporary basis and with proof of the threat of serious harm to national production.

Import duties range from zero to 20 percent, and the 10-percent value-added tax applies to most imports. Nontariff barriers consist mainly of import licensing, import quotas, and exchange controls. The government has sought to eliminate license requirements for certain imports, and further liberalization will take place under NAFTA. Import quotas vary from year to year, depending on national production of many basic grains. Items subject to the quotas include basic grains, oilseeds, milk products, and coffee.[54]

Mexico is also attempting to forge closer trade links with the rest of Latin America, as demonstrated by signing a bilateral free trade agreement with Chile, cooperating within the Group of Three (Mexico, Colombia, and Venezuela), and planning for integration with Central America. However, Brazil and Argentina remain Mexico's most important trading partners in Latin America, while the United States purchases over three quarters of Mexico's exports, provides nearly the same proportion of its imports, and is the largest source of FDI in Mexico (contributing 63 percent in 1996).

U.S. Corporate Presence

Traditionally, U.S. corporate presence in Mexico has been concentrated in the manufacturing sector, with the majority of investments in the automotive, computer, and *maquiladora* (manufacturing, processing and/or assembling U.S. parts that are shipped back to the United States) industries. During the past decade, however, U.S. investment has shifted toward financial services.

Maquiladoras

In the import-substitution development era, the northern border region between Mexico and the United States — a market flooded by readily available U.S. commodities — lagged in economic progress compared to all other regions. In the mid-1960s, seeking to attract U.S. assembly plants, the administration of President Gustavo Díaz Ordaz (1964-1970) announced the Border Industrialization Program (BIP). The BIP allowed foreign and Mexican investors temporarily to import duty free all inputs, machinery, and replacement parts needed for assembly as long as the investors purchased bonds ensuring their eventual reexportation. The government referred to plants set up under the BIP as maquiladoras, although a legal framework for them was not created until 1971.[55] These regulations granted full foreign ownership, while further tax exemptions from the U.S. Tariff Schedules promoted their implementation. Currently, maquiladoras are listed under tariff provisions 9802.00.60 and 9802.00.80 of the Harmonized Tariff System.

Manufacturers that assemble or process U.S. components abroad for reexport to the United States are subject to duties that are levied effectively only on that portion of a product's value that is added abroad, not on a product's final value. Half of the value added to goods in Mexico is labor input; because of low Mexican wages, maquiladoras gain an advantage in international markets.[56]

During Mexico's earlier economic crisis of 1982, the maquiladora sector was the only sector of the economy that continued to grow, due to its export-oriented production and because regular devaluations of the peso made Mexican wages very competitive.[57] The de la Madrid administration's 1983 Maquiladora Decree sought to promote the industry primarily as a source of foreign exchange and jobs but also as a way to catalyze industrial development.[58] The decree permitted maquiladoras to sell up to 20 percent of their production in domestic markets as long as no competing Mexican commodities were available. The decree also made the establishment of a maquiladora easier by creating a single administrative entity to supervise the industry. During this period, the maquiladoras produced more foreign exchange than any other sector of the economy, including tourism, except for petroleum.[59]

The Salinas administration's 1989 Maquiladora Decree stated explicitly that it would seek to integrate the maquiladora sector more fully into the national economy. The decree permitted the maquiladoras to sell one-third of their production in Mexico without the previous restrictions as long as they maintained a positive foreign currency account and exempted Mexican suppliers of maquiladoras from the value-added tax.[60] Maquiladoras are now viewed as a "priority component of a national development strategy aimed at the external market."[61]

This change in the perception of the maquiladoras is a result of a change in structure within the industry itself. Worker productivity has increased, production is more capital intensive, and many maquiladoras now carry on higher valued-added manufacturing along with assembly. Furthermore, women are no longer the main maquiladora employees, working with low value-added assembly activity.[62] Similarly, since 1983, maquiladoras in the interior of the country have grown faster than those along the border, which increased the maquiladoras' share of the total Mexican manufacturing sector workforce to about 20 percent by 1988.[63] The government wanted to expand maquiladoras in the interior to increase the use of domestic raw and intermediate inputs, such as electric and electronic equipment. Foreign firms were also searching for "more integrated clusters of suppliers in their overseas locations."[64] If Mexico could achieve such "clusters," it would be even more attractive to foreign investors in regions of the interior that are still in early stages of industrialization.

Still, despite recent efforts, less than 2 percent of an annual total of some $20 billion in raw and intermediate materials used by the maquiladora sector are purchased in Mexico, reflecting very weak linkages between export-oriented industries and the rest of the Mexican economy.[65] While the second generation of maquiladoras is more vertically integrated, employs more technicians, engineers, and managers, and uses more advanced technology, foreign-owned maquiladoras in the interior have failed to create large supplier networks.[66]

Although maquiladoras will not solve all of Mexico's economic problems, they have grown constantly since their establishment. According to a recent study by the Wharton Econometrics Forecasting Association, maquiladora exports rose from $5 billion in 1992 to an estimated $17.3 billion in 1997. Similarly, the value of total production increased from $19.8 billion in 1992 to an estimated 67.6 billion in 1997. The sector's growth rate is impressive: the maquiladora industry has grown at an average annual rate of 23.4 percent, if measured in terms of number of plants (from 12 in 1966 to 1,500 in 1989, 1,850 in 1993, and 2,100 in 1995). If measured in terms of total number of employees, the average annual growth rate is 23 percent (from 3,000 in 1966 to 350,000 in 1989, 522,000 in 1995, and an estimated 1.154 million by the end of 1997).[67] In terms of sectoral representation, 26 percent of all maquiladoras are in electronics; 22 percent in automotive; 18 percent in services (credit card and airline ticket processing); 13 percent in textiles and apparel; 11 percent in electrical appliances; 6 percent in wood products; and 4 percent in chemicals.[68]

Prior to NAFTA, the maquiladora sector could not sell more than 50 percent of the total value of a previous year's annual exports to the domestic market. In 1995, this increased to 60 percent; in 1996, to 65 percent; and in 1997, to 70 percent. In 1998, it will be 80 percent, and all restrictions on domestic sales will be lifted by year end 2001.

Under NAFTA, the maquiladora sector is expected to lose much of its unique appeal since incentives to encourage export sales, such as in-bond facilities, will be eliminated. These changes in tax legislation and the overall impact of NAFTA will force maquiladoras to revise how they view themselves and to adopt new strategies for the future — in particular, to continue the shift to more capital-intensive operations. Asian companies, still a minority among the overwhelming number of U.S. and Canadian operations along the border, are leading this development. For instance, the electronics arms of Goldstar and Samsung, Korean firms with maquila facilities in Mexicali and Tijuana, are now increasing capacity and expanding their range of products.

Most maquiladoras now in operation seem prepared to stay on. Having developed infrastructure, local expertise, plants, and facilities, they are adapting by employing more Mexican workers in middle and senior management and implementing more capital-intensive operations. This is where the maquiladoras' big potential now lies. In this way, they will become more like foreign companies already established outside the existing maquiladora framework.

Automobiles

For President Salinas, the automotive industry represented "Mexico's plans to establish itself as a serious manufacturing competitor on the global stage."[69] In 1962, the automotive sector was a highly regulated industry, in which 10 companies produced only 67,000 cars a year. Nonetheless, despite restrictions, automotive sales increased by roughly 32 percent a year between 1962 and 1982, while employment rose in the same period by 69 percent a year.[70] Today, Mexico is the second largest automotive market in Latin America. Almost 600,000 cars were sold there in 1994, up 3.7 percent from 1993. According to the U.S. Department of Commerce, the Mexican market will reach 1 million units by the year 2000 and 1.5 million units by 2010.[71]

In the late 1980s, the Ford Motor Company pioneered a new course that other companies, such as Nissan and Volkswagen, would follow. Ford's main problem was the high cost of parts imported from Japan. It had expanded its plant in Hermosillo, Sonora, from a 130,000 unit capacity in 1984 to 170,000 in 1989 and lowered its production costs by importing 75 percent of its parts from the United States. Ford's investments in Hermosillo had come on line in 1987, and by 1989 Ford was exporting 75 percent of its Mexican cars, achieving a $1.7 billion surplus.[72] These results, together with parallel development by Chrysler and General Motors, demonstrated to the Mexican government that the exporting capacity of the automotive company was crucial to its prosperity.

Growth in the automotive sector resulted in the 1989 Automotive Decree, which further liberalized the conditions for operating in the sector. The Decree allowed automakers to import cars and trucks for the first time in 30 years. Vehicle manufacturers could produce as many different models in Mexico as they desired, unencumbered by government restrictions, and could freely select their autoparts suppliers, whether Mexican or foreign.[73]

By 1989, more than 80 percent of Mexico's vehicle exports went to the United States. Mexico had accounted for 13 percent of U.S. autoparts imports and was the largest source of automotive exports to the United States after Japan and Canada. In 1995, total motor vehicle exports to Mexico reached $394 million, which represented 1.9 percent of total U.S. motor vehicle trade. Mexico had become America's third largest trading partner in an increasingly integrated North American economic system — well before NAFTA, in large part because of automotive exports.[74]

Computers

The computer industry occupied a special place in Salinas' modernization plan — similar to the auto sector in that it provided competitive advantages to the service sector and promoted the integration of Mexico in the global economy. In 1996, the computer market reached $2.5 billion (the second largest market in Latin America and sixteenth largest in the world) and is expected to grow to $5.27 billion by 2000. According to estimates by trade experts, the market is expected to grow 14 percent per year over the next several years.[75] To date, PC and workstation sales are growing twice as fast as mainframes and represent over 80 percent of the computer market (up from 66 percent in 1991). The software market, 75 percent of which is supplied by U.S. firms, has also grown at a double digit rate over the past three years to $400 million in 1994.

Before 1981, all computers sold in Mexico were imported. In order to encourage domestic investment in the computer industry, a 1981 decree required firms seeking to supply the Mexican market to set up local manufacturing facilities. The decree also stipulated that the firms must be established with 51-percent Mexican ownership.

In 1985, however, the Mexican government granted 100-percent ownership to IBM, due to problems in the Mexican economy and IBM's promise to increase its Mexican investment in the proposed plant from $6.6 million to $91 million over a five-year period.[76] Consequently, the computer industry experienced its greatest growth between 1982 and 1989, averaging 52.2 percent annually. Export sales also increased impressively, in 1989 registering $380 million in sales of IBM computer products. These developments showed the government that further liberalization in the computer industry — as in the maquiladora and automotive sectors — was needed for the industry to keep developing.[77]

The 1990 Computer Decree was issued with three key objectives: to increase the competitiveness of the computer industry, to enhance the competitiveness of those who rely on computers to achieve superior performance, and to offer Mexican consumers the widest possible variety of state-of-the-art computer hardware and software at internationally competitive prices.[78] Once again, longtime investors were protected by the decree from new investors, especially in the area of imports.[79]

Mexico provides a classic example of how foreign companies at times can favor foreign investment regulations — when they are large enough to be able to afford significant concessions and thereby gain large, guaranteed market shares. IBM, which was permitted to open a wholly owned subsidiary in Mexico when the company increased its investment, as described above, stimulated the growth of local suppliers and set up a development and a semiconductor research center. Other foreign computer companies, including Hewlett-Packard, Burroughs, Apple, and Honeywell, opposed IBM's deal, complaining that IBM was allowed 100 percent ownership for concessions it could not provide. Furthermore, the other companies feared that if IBM produced the quantities it promised, it would oversupply the market and overpower prior competitors.[80] Mexico did grant additional concessions to IBM's competitors.

Banking and Financial Services

The most restricted sector of the Mexican economy for foreign investors has been banking and financial services. The trend is beginning to change, however, with the liberalization of the economy and the passage of NAFTA. The domestic banking system was nationalized under President López Portillo in 1982 to halt the dollar drain, but it had the opposite effect. Foreign investors fled, as did some $80 billion in Mexican capital. President Salinas decided to reverse this decision, reprivatizing the banking sector in an effort to increase foreign and local investors' confidence.[81] By 1992, almost all of the 18 Mexican banks had been sold.[82] In order to consolidate the industry, improve service, and increase concurrence, 14 new banks were licensed between 1993 and 1994, raising the number of banks to 34. However, in early 1994, the largest three banks held 53 percent of all loans and 59 percent of commercial banking system capital.

Another key element of liberalization has been the formation of financial groups in Mexico. Since individual investors are banned from owning more than 5 percent of a bank's shares, financial groups are an alternative. They can own 100 percent of a commercial bank. The 1990 law allows financial firms to merge under a single financial group.[83] Foreign participation is still restricted to 30 percent of a bank's equity, but this will eventually grow, particularly in areas such as corporate finance and investment banking, although retail banking will probably emerge as a local activity.[84] As of 1997, foreigners were limited to 1.5 percent of the banking system's total capital.[85] Joint market share can increase to 15 percent in 1999. By the year 2000, such regulations will be abolished, except in emergency cases.

The U.S. corporate presence in Mexico, then, has grown and broadened over the years in response to domestic, regional, and global forces. The maquiladoras have received notable attention, although automobiles, computers, and financial services have also expanded, affecting and being affected by economic moderation.

Conclusion

The experiences of Canada and Mexico with late twentieth-century industrialization and economic growth are distinct, especially with regard to levels of development and inter-state relations. Canada is a highly industrialized, wealthy, politically and economically democratic, and culturally "Northern" nation. Although long concerned to defend its economic and cultural autonomy, Canada has benefited greatly from its unique and intimate relationship with the United States. Mexico's experiences, in contrast, traditionally have been those of a developing, poor, semi-democratic, and economically stratified nation, whose relations with the United States have been shaped by a history of conflict, confrontation, tension, and exploitation.

Yet, there are also important parallels between the two countries. During the 1970s in particular, nationalist governments in Ottawa and Mexico City sought to leverage the windfall profits from the rise in oil prices to create economic systems that would be more autonomous in the global economy and more independent of the United States. In 1982, these aspirations collapsed in both countries. By mid-decade, Canadian and Mexican leaders had come to realize that the only viable alternative was the formation of some sort of North American economic arrangement. Since then, both countries have experienced a remarkable shift in economic policy orientation; both have pursued policies of economic liberalization, including privatizing state enterprises, striving to reduce governmental deficits, and reducing barriers to foreign investment. Both have seen the end of elaborate systems of branch plants and the integration of many foreign-owned (mainly U.S.) operations into cross-border networks that no longer focus primarily on national economies. One of the few studies that compares economic development in Mexico and Canada, conducted by Thomas Legler, concludes in this fashion, "During the twenty-five odd years following the Second World War, Canada and Mexico enjoyed a relative prosperity underpinned by remarkably similar models of economic growth. In the course of post-war development their economies have become increasingly functionally integrated. It can only be hoped that the present course of economic convergence will lead to a brighter future for both countries."[86]

Chapter Three

An Emerging North American Economy: Corporate Strategy

"Canada" and "Mexico" were key strategic and operational concepts for U.S. firms through the early 1980s. In resource sectors, U.S. mining and petroleum companies provided critical links between domestic resource production and global markets. In manufacturing industries, import-substitution strategies compelled U.S. firms to establish branch plants. These branch operations enjoyed protected national markets for selling their goods and faced a wide range of pressures to increase benefits to the host economy by importing less, exporting more, hiring more local managers, enhancing local value-added activities, and carrying out more research and development. Each host country offered a particular mix of incentives to encourage foreign firms to meet national objectives.

The Canadian and Mexican governments sought to balance national interests and objectives as well as market forces, including intensifying international competition, technological innovation, and falling resource prices. These same market forces were also reshaping corporate structures and strategies. Increasingly, corporate strategies shaped rather than followed government policies. Corporate strategies that rationalized and integrated North American operations pressed governments to liberalize their economies further, while liberalization encouraged the formation of an increasingly dense network of cross-border ties.

In Canada, U.S. firms had responded to growing regulatory and political pressures in the 1970s by increasing local content in their own operations and raising levels of Canadian autonomy within corporate structures. This meant more Canadian inputs at all stages of the production process and a stronger role for Canadian managers in decisionmaking. At the same time, the level of protection in the Canadian market was falling substantially in the course of successive GATT Rounds, and freer trade and heightened global competition were altering the basic framework of bilateral relations and the foundation on which corporate structures and strategies in Canada and North America would stand. The result was that efforts to Canadianize and localize operations — to be "good Canadian corporate citizens" — were overwhelmed by the need to respond to intensified international competition in an environment in which national borders were less and less important for defining economic boundaries. U.S. firms in an increasingly integrated U.S.-Canadian economy sought ways to reduce costs by rationalizing and integrating their sourcing, production, and distribution systems.

The response of U.S. multinational firms in Mexico to this emerging environment paralleled experiences of U.S. subsidiaries in Canada during the 1970s. With multinational companies and international agencies, such as the World Bank, providing the lion's share of capital Mexico needed to finance investment, Mexican nationalism, long antipathetic toward U.S. direct investment, was tempered with a new pragmatism, ensuring the continued inflow of investment. Multinational firms tailored their strategies, structures, and operations in Mexico to the dual realities of an older, restricted, regulated, protectionist, import-substitution economy and an emerging, competitive, liberal, open, export-oriented economy. Consumer goods and information technology manufacturers, for example, had enjoyed oligopolistic profits due to high tariffs on imports. Consequently, the liberalization of the Mexican economy forced multinational subsidiaries to increase efficiency, contend with slimmer profit margins, shift production to exports, and rationalize and integrate their operations vis-à-vis headquarters and other subsidiaries.

As in the case of Canada, efforts had been made to Mexicanize and localize operations; these were not abandoned but rather *recast*. Mexican demographics (a high population growth rate, an expansion of the economically active population, and an expanding middle class) fueled an ever increasing demand for consumer durables and non-durables. Consequently, the Mexicanization and localization of U.S. subsidiaries — especially the sales, marketing, and advertising functions — advanced corporate interests in Mexico and coexisted with internationalization.

Liberalization was not a source of immediate benefits for all firms. U.S. firms operating in Mexico with sufficient market power to enable them to come to terms with Mexican regulations and to meet national needs in exchange for market reservations found themselves facing new competitors. Similarly, U.S. operations in Canada were often faced with excess capacity because of the emergence of continental strategies and the end of protected branch plants.

Changes in corporate strategy and structure in North America have two key dimensions. The first is the integration of the Canadian and, somewhat more slowly, Mexican subsidiaries of U.S. firms into more or less coherent continental systems. The second is the rationalization of production capacity and workforces, which has preceded and typically intensified integration. These efforts to rationalize and integrate U.S., Canadian, and Mexican business operations seem to be moving forward rapidly and are accompanied by high levels of organizational innovation and experimentation.

Corporate Strategy

On the eve of CUSFTA, well-known Canadian scholars Joseph D'Cruz and James Fleck studied how U.S. subsidiaries in Canada were responding to globalization and projected how they might react to the impending free trade agreement. They concluded that a Canada-U.S. free trade agreement would intensify the pressure on U.S. firms to deploy their resources across the continent more efficiently, just as developments in Europe were driving forward pan-European integration and rationalization:

> There can be little doubt that similar forces will be put into play when the Free Trade agreement between Canada and the U.S. is implemented. For one thing, intra-firm trade is already well established between the two countries. Thus, the administrative infrastructure for rationalization of production between the U.S. and Canadian operations already exists in many U.S. multinationals. For most, the

next round of major capital projects is highly likely to involve more rationalization between production facilities in Canada and the U.S.[87]

Research carried out in the three linked studies, undertaken by The Conference Board of Canada, the Americas Society, and the North-South Center, indicates clearly that D'Cruz and Fleck's projections were on target. The great majority of respondents in the surveys, all of whom were managers in U.S. firms with long established operations in Mexico and Canada, agreed that CUSFTA and NAFTA intensified trends already underway toward the development of continental-wide strategies and the creation of North American production, marketing, and sourcing networks. A quotation from CPC International's Annual Report for 1990 illustrates clearly how the free trade agreement intensified trends already underway: "Corn refining operations in North America also benefited from a realignment of existing businesses in the U.S. and Canada, which allows the company to capitalize on opportunities accompanying the free trade agreement between the two countries. Further coordination between CPC's U.S. and Canadian corn refining businesses will be achieved as trade barriers between the countries continue to fall."[88]

An Emerging North American Focus

In this and subsequent chapters, we review the findings of the three linked studies and rely primarily on data obtained from questionnaire surveys of headquarters managers of U.S. firms and of managers of U.S. subsidiaries in Mexico. Managers from 52 firms took part in this research (see Appendix for listing). These data are supplemented by materials from the 1992 Conference Board of Canada project as well as by in-depth interviews with many of the questionnaire respondents and documentary research.

In our questionnaire survey of U.S. headquarters and Mexican subsidiary managers, we asked first if their firms had adopted or considered adopting a North American focus in their corporate strategy and structure. Table 1 shows that 70 percent of the firms in the 1994 Americas Society survey of U.S. headquarters managers reported that their firms had already done so or were currently considering doing so. A further 17 percent said that they had not moved in this direction but were likely to do so in the near future. Only four of the 34 responding firms either had rejected or not considered the idea.

Table 1.

Has your firm assumed a North American focus in its strategy and structure? U.S. Headquarters Respondents

(n=34)	No. of Firms	% of Respondents
Yes, definitely	17	50.0
Currently considering	7	20.5
Not yet, but likely to do so	6	17.6
No, rejected the idea	3	8.8
No, not considered the idea	1	2.9

Source: *U.S. Firms in North America: Redefining Structure and Strategy, North American Outlook*, 1995 (Americas Society study).

The results of our 1994-1996 survey of U.S. subsidiaries in Mexico, illustrated in Table 2, show an even more powerful confirmation of the shift to a North-South orientation of trade and economic links. Fully 80 percent of the respondents said their firms had already adopted a North American focus in their corporate structure and strategy. Six percent said they were currently considering this prospect, and a further 6 percent said they were likely to move in this direction. Only 6 percent said they had not considered the idea, and none of the responding firms had rejected it completely.

Table 2.

Has your firm assumed a North American focus in its strategy and structure? Mexican Subsidiary Respondents

(n=31)	No. of Firms	%
Yes, definitely	25	80.1
Currently considering	2	6.5
Not yet, but likely to do so	2	6.5
No, rejected the idea	0	0.0
No, not considered the idea	2	6.5

Source: North-South Center study, 1994-1996.

It is important to underscore that definitions of "North America" differed among the respondent firms. While most included Mexico in their vision of "North America," some did not. (One or two included the Caribbean.) Reorganization typically focused initially on Canada and the United States, where high levels of integration were already in place, including close relationships between assemblers and suppliers, and where a highly developed transportation and communication infrastructure facilitated integration. The United States and Canada also share a common language (except in Quebec) and a similar business culture. And in many industries, products are similar or identical.

A large majority of respondents said that their firms were moving toward some sort of North American strategic orientation. We sought evidence of actual change, such as substantial changes in relations between U.S. headquarters and their Canadian and Mexican subsidiaries. When we asked whether there had been significant change in the relationship with the respondent's firm and its Canadian or Mexican operations over the past five years, almost 70 percent of all respondents — 68 percent of U.S. headquarters respondents and 69 percent of the Mexican respondents — reported that such changes had taken place.

Table 3.

Over the past five years, has there been a significant change in the relationship with your firm's Canadian operations?

U.S. Headquarters Respondents

(n=34)	No. of Firms	%
Yes	23	67.7
No	10	29.4
Not applicable	1	2.9

Source: *U.S. Firms in North America: Redefining Structure and Strategy, North American Outlook*, 1995 (Americas Society study).

Responses indicated a level of change in the relationship of U.S. parents and their Canadian and Mexican subsidiaries that was much greater than most experts seem to have expected.[89]

Table 4.

Over the past five years, has there been a significant change in the relationship with your firm's Mexican operations?

Mexican Subsidiary Respondents

(n=36)	No. of firms	%
Yes	25	69.4
No	11	31.6
Not applicable	0	0.0

Source: North-South Center study, 1994-1995.

Another survey of foreign-owned subsidiaries in Canada, conducted for The Conference Board of Canada by Gilles Rheaume and Jacek Ward in 1994, found that 42 percent of its respondents said that their firms had experienced a change in the relationship with their parents over the previous five years. Some 58 percent reported no change.[90] This is a smaller percentage than was reported in our surveys. The reasons for the difference are probably because some of the respondents were in the automotive sector, in which integration had been underway since the U.S.-Canada Auto Pact in the 1960s, and others were in wholesale and retail trade, which were much less affected by the free trade agreement. Only 60 percent of the firms participating in this Conference Board survey were U.S.-based, and this may have influenced the outcome as well. Still, these caveats notwithstanding, the fact that almost half of the respondents in such a wide-ranging survey reported a substantial change in the relations with their foreign parents in the previous five years is remarkable.

We then asked what kind of change had taken place in these relationships. Respondents who reported that significant change in the relationship between U.S.

headquarters and Canadian (Table 5) and Mexican (Table 6) subsidiaries had taken place were asked to describe what had happened. U.S. headquarters respondents replied that the direction of change was overwhelmingly toward greater integration of the Canadian and U.S. operations. Four of the 32 respondents who reported significant change in the relationship with their Canadian subsidiaries said that these operations had been integrated into the U.S. entity or into U.S. product lines. Eight reported that they had been integrated into a North American entity and seven into North American or global product lines. Two said that they had closed Canadian operations, and three said that they had opened new Canadian headquarters (see Table 5).

Table 5.

If there has been significant change between your firm and its Canadian affiliate, what has occurred to change the relationship significantly?
U.S. Headquarters Respondents

(n=32)	No. of Mentions
Established a new Canadian headquarters	3
Integrated operations into a U.S. entity	2
Integrated operations into a North American entity	8
Integrated operations into U.S. product divisions	2
Integrated operations into North American product divisions	4
Integrated operations into global product divisions	3
Closed Canadian operations	2
Other	8

Source: *U.S. Firms in North America: Redefining Structure and Strategy,*
North American Outlook, 1995 (Americas Society study).

Mexican responses indicated even more clearly that the major drive is toward greater integration of North American operations. Nearly half of the 35 respondents who reported a significant change in the relationship with their Mexican subsidiary said that the Mexican operations had been integrated into some sort of U.S. or North American entity or product division (see Table 6).

Four of the Mexican subsidiaries had been integrated into the U.S. business organization and two into U.S. product divisions. Six became part of a North American business entity, and 12 became part of either North American or global product divisions. No Mexican operations had been closed, and six new headquarters had opened.

Though the number of responses is small and we are not certain that each of them uses these terms in exactly the same way, we can still see several tentative conclusions emerge. A certain number of U.S. firms, a minority of the whole sample but not an insignificant one, collapsed their Canadian or Mexican subsidiaries into the U.S. operations. A somewhat larger number of firms integrated their Canadian and, to a lesser extent, their Mexican operations into a (often new) North American division, and about the same number restructured their operations into either North American or global product divisions. Few companies closed down their operations in Mexico or Canada.

Table 6.

If there has been significant change between your firm and its Mexican affiliate, what has occurred to change the relationship significantly? Mexican Subsidiary Respondents

(n=35)	No. of Mentions
Established a new Mexican headquarters	6
Integrated operations into a U.S. entity	4
Integrated operations into a North American entity	6
Integrated operations into U.S. product divisions	2
Integrated operations into North American product divisions	5
Integrated operations into global product divisions	7
Closed Mexican operations	0
Other	5

Source: North-South Center study, 1994-1996.

The differences in the responses between Canadian and Mexican affiliates may be attributed to the level of development of the Canadian subsidiaries in contrast to their Mexican counterparts. The integration of Mexican operations into a global product division is a relatively recent phenomenon. Many Canadian subsidiaries had already achieved global involvements, some as a result of earlier pressure on U.S. headquarters to give Canadian affiliates "world product mandates." The period of the early 1990s was a time of awakening on the part of U.S. multinationals with respect to the need for a significant presence in Mexico and for existing Mexican affiliates to deepen and expand their activities vis-à-vis both the U.S. and world markets. As a top manager of Honeywell asserted, "Reevaluation of the Mexican market caused a 180-degree change in the firm's thinking. 'Global thinking' is the centerpiece of our new, corporate culture, and Mexico's potential is tremendous."[91] The establishment of new Mexican headquarters and the integration of operations into a U.S. entity are recent developments. These steps had begun among Canadian affiliates two decades earlier.

Companies have utilized a number of strategies to enter the Mexican market and align their home-base operations with it. The strategic response varies with each company and greatly depends on the individual firm's corporate culture, size, product line (also called division), and existing presence in Mexico. Some companies, such as Xerox, said that Mexico will become a site for global sourcing. In labor-intensive industries, companies might want to move to Mexico to take advantage of low labor costs. Others may decide to pull out investments or downsize operations in Mexico in the wake of the removal of import restrictions, preferring to service the market through distributors instead.[92]

Firms have responded to these new conditions by paying greater attention to product quality and customer service. Companies that have not achieved world quality standards under protected markets in Mexico are being forced to implement quality improvement programs. Others have rationalized operations and markets regionally to achieve economies of scale, worked more closely with local suppliers, invested in technology and the development of new products, made use of liberalized regulations to effect technology transfer, created a North American division, and created new strategic alliances, mergers and acquisitions, or regained majority control of subsidiaries. Some, including several Asian companies, have relocated operations from Asian sites to Mexico to take advantage of NAFTA access to North American markets.[93] As a Singer executive pointed out: "We clearly want to export more to the U.S., particularly higher end production, since certain product lines are still cheaper to import from Asia than to manufacture here or import from the U.S."[94]

Several companies highlighted below provide interesting and representative examples of the trend toward continental integration. These examples contain information derived in the course of our survey research, much of which has not been published previously.

CAMPBELL SOUP

Until a few years before NAFTA, the Campbell Soup Company's branch plant operations in Canada and Mexico reflected the parent company in virtually all aspects of business. Decentralized decisionmaking encouraged Canadian and Mexican managers to tailor products to local markets but inhibited cross-border strategies. Intensifying competition, deteriorating financial performance, and a growing concern about operating inefficiencies, together with new leadership at the top of the company, led Campbell to a series of critical organizational changes. When he became the new CEO in 1991, David Johnson sought to create a corporate structure that could take advantage of an emerging North American market that would generate vigorous growth for the firm's core products. Johnson observed, "People point to the European market of 325 million people. But there's truly greater potential in a single North American market of more than 364 million people today, and more than 400 million by the year 2000."[95]

The rich North American market would be the hub of Campbell's global strategy. As Johnson stated, "The North American Common Market, as I call it, will be funding our initiatives across the oceans."[96] Johnson began to consolidate Canadian and Mexican operations with the U.S. business into Campbell North America. A Campbell North American Division was created to tap into the powers of the Canada-U.S. common market.

The transition was not easy. Johnson had to merge three separate national entities into a unified production system glued together by a common strategic vision. His strategic vision was not complicated: "The strategy for North America is very simple. You market locally, manufacture regionally, and source globally — with common technology, knowledge and supplies."[97]

3M

At 3M, a large, U.S.-based consumer and industrial products firm, the international division no longer has a role in Mexican operations. All business units in Canada and Mexico now deal directly with 3M divisions in the United States. The company has also redefined the functions of managers in Canada and Mexico, who now serve as the main links between local customers and general managers in the United States. Canadian and Mexican managers also work directly with the planning, pricing, and operating teams at headquarters. These redefined management functions are necessary as 3M synchronizes new product launches and coordinates distribution strategies, with the aim of achieving standardization in sizing and parts numbers and uniformity in sales literature, packaging, and labeling. As of 1994, 3M had established a single system to handle North American accounts and was working to harmonize prices across borders. Plans were undertaken to share technical equipment and personnel and to organize joint training. Mexico's role in production was slated to be strengthened in the coming years. The Mexican subsidiary was to become a site for some new-product launches, suppliers to the maquiladoras (3M's sales to in-bond plants are currently handled by U.S. divisions), and a growing center for the company's manufacturing.

WHIRLPOOL

Whirlpool tells a similar story. In 1988, the company's top management decided that by integrating the Canadian, Mexican, and U.S. markets into "an encompassing, unified vision," they would be able to "capitalize on the proven success of individual brands while taking advantage of economies of scale through an integrated manufacturing network and better leverage limited resources in a highly competitive market."[98] The objective of the company's new North American Appliance Group, according to Executive Vice President William Marohn in 1991, was to improve manufacturing efficiency and cost effectiveness in all of its North American operations.[99]

In the late 1980s, Whirlpool formed a joint venture, named Vitromatic, with Mexican glass maker Vitro. The shift in lines of control moved from Whirlpool's international division, where Vitromatic's managers formerly reported, to its North American group. Vitromatic received technical and managerial support from Whirlpool's U.S. operations and acted as an importer of U.S.-made products and an exporter of appliances to the United States.

GENERAL ELECTRIC

General Electric (GE) greatly expanded its activity in Asia and Mexico. However, while the majority of GE operations in Asia are aimed at serving local markets, the case is different for Mexico. Before the passage of NAFTA, GE began fully integrating Mexico into its emerging North American manufacturing strategy. Low labor costs drove it to build a factory in 1990 in San Luis Potosí to produce gas ranges, and production grew to account for a considerable percentage of gas ranges in the United States. The facility is a joint venture with Mabe, a Mexican appliance maker. The partnership also includes a $7 million research and development center. Similar to the organizational structure at 3M and Whirlpool, which give the country's operations an immediate link to the home office, local Mexican executives report directly to GE's appliance chiefs in Louisville, Kentucky, not to a GE country manager in Mexico. When added to GE's longtime Mexican presence and desire to serve the fast growing local market, it is apparent how important Mexico is to the company. This is reflected in the structure of management training for its Mexico personnel. GE's training programs, which focus on lean management, quick response, fast product cycles, and productivity, have been exported to its Mexican operations. In a new program, Mexican middle managers are rotated through different assignments for two years while studying at night. Though common in the United States, programs of this kind are new to Mexico. In the United States, new managerial hires are given courses in global issues at GE's training center in Crotonville, New York.

XEROX

Xerox provides another example of changes in organizational structure within a North American context. For 30 years, this company enjoyed a monopoly in Mexico. In 1986 the opening started, and Xerox could no longer take advantage of a closed market. The firm had to shift from a cash cow to a market orientation. It developed much closer relations with suppliers, intensified its use and sale of the latest technologies, and initiated an expansion of credit to its customer bases. Globalization was underway, and the company had to reassess its cost-expense structure, engage in greater competitive analysis, and focus more on an entirely new planning and analytical operation. Xerox never really had to compete before in Mexico, having enjoyed a captive market. The company realized that with tariff barriers falling, gross margins dropping, and price differentiation between the United States and Mexico narrowing, it would have to make a concerted effort to compete.

The magnitude of change within corporate networks, along the lines suggested in the above examples, is still surprising to most observers. These trends toward greater integration are not new; they were well underway before the CUSFTA or NAFTA but seem to have accelerated over the past few years.[100]

The drive to integrate Mexican operations with those in Canada and the United States is not a strategy that works for everyone. Existing corporate organization was an issue in some cases. In several companies such as CPC and Kodak, the Mexican subsidiary reported to the firm's Latin American division. Strong personal feelings as well as organizational concerns inhibited major changes in structure. Motorola found that it benefited from keeping Mexican operations under its Latin American umbrella. Mexican management in this case believed that its Latin American customers appreciated a strong Latin orientation; the firm was reluctant, therefore, to integrate its Mexican operations into a North American operation.[101] Here, and in other firms as well, the direction of cross-border integration might be southward, from Mexico. All of these reasons made integration into a North American business unit more difficult in practical terms, however desirable in theory.

The Anglo-Dutch Unilever has felt no need to create a North American division up to this time. Management determined that its global focus could adapt to the changes in North America. David Lustig, a U.S.-based manager, observed, "It does not look probable that we would begin to integrate Canadian and U.S. manufacturing capacity. Perhaps if NAFTA were as radical an undertaking as EC '92, then we would have to consider it."[102] The firm reported that it was considering some sort of North American focus and that its leaders felt that additional benefits could be obtained by creating a North American group. Affiliates in Canada and the United States have increased communication and cooperation because of CUSFTA — especially in the area of information exchange and R&D. The affiliates also assist each other in their production strategies. Subsidiaries still produce for their own national markets, but there is more flexibility in their strategies. Nevertheless, a drastic overhaul in structure or strategy was not contemplated by Unilever at this time.[103]

Gillette responded to these same pressures in a much different fashion. Until 1988, the company was structured along North American lines. It managed its Canadian and U.S. operations under a unified North American division, although each country had its own separate production facilities. The North American division oversaw marketing and advertising in the two countries. In 1989, the North American division was subsumed into a North Atlantic Group in order to gain efficiencies in marketing, advertising, and promotions. Gillette felt that its products were global and could be sold in different markets using essentially the same advertising and marketing strategies. At the same time, Gillette began to supply the entire Canadian and U.S. markets from a single U.S.-based plant, closing its higher cost Canadian production facility.

As these cases illustrate, the trend toward continental integration is shaped by a firm's historical presence in national markets, regional objectives, existing organizational arrangements, global competitive challenges, and the dynamic relationship among all of these factors.

Chapter Four

Continental Integration and Rationalization: Corporate Perspectives

For this study, we asked respondents what objectives their firms sought from North American integration and rationalization strategies. The responses overwhelmingly emphasized improving bottom-line performance on a North American scale. While few Mexican or Canadian subsidiary managers disagreed with these priorities, many were still concerned about the impact of these changes on their operations. In this chapter, we explore concerns, fears, and reasons surrounding rationalization strategies.

What Did Firms Hope to Gain?

U.S. corporate headquarters respondents to the Americas Society survey and respondents to the North-South Center survey of subsidiaries in Mexico were asked what goals their companies hoped to achieve as a result of their firms' initiatives to integrate their North American operations. Responses in the two surveys were basically similar, with a few interesting differences.

Answers cluster among several goals for Canadian subsidiaries (see Table 7). Three of the four objectives for Canadian operations mentioned most frequently by headquarters executives focus on improving the bottom line: increasing the profitability of Canadian operations, expanding market share in Canada, and increasing the volume of Canadian business operations. Twenty-six of the 32 respondents also said that, over the next few years, their firms hope to integrate Canadian operations into some sort of U.S., North American, or global network.

Table 7.
As your firm looks toward the next several years, what are the major goals it hopes to accomplish in Canada? U.S. Headquarters Respondents

(n=32)	No. of Mentions
Increase profitability	22
Heighten Canadian identity of business	6
Increase market share	22
Increase volume of Canadian operations	20
Increase lines of business	6
Reduce lines of business	1
Integrate operations into U.S./North American networks	19
Integrate operations into global networks	7
Reduce overheads of Canadian operations	12
Close Canadian operations	0

Source: *U.S. Firms in North America: Redefining Structure and Strategy,* 1995 (Americas Society study).

33

None of the 32 respondents to this question lists closing down Canadian operations as a goal. Only one mentions reducing lines of business among the firm's goals — a clear difference from responses at the Canadian subsidiary level, when The Conference Board survey one year earlier showed high levels of concern about closing down business operations. Twelve of those polled for the Americas Society study say their firms will try to reduce overheads in Canada. Few will seek to heighten the Canadian identity of their operations in Canada, which was a key goal for many U.S. subsidiaries in Canada in the 1970s.

In Mexico, this question elicited similar responses (see Table 8). The most frequently mentioned objectives for Mexican subsidiaries are the same as for subsidiary operations in Canada: increase the volume of Mexican operations, expand market share in Mexico, and increase the profitability of Mexican operations. The shift toward a North American strategy is basically aimed at improving the bottom line.

Table 8.
As your firm looks toward the next several years, what are the major goals it hopes to accomplish in Mexico? Mexico Subsidiary Respondents

(n=37)	No. of Mentions
Increase profitability	21
Heighten Mexican identity of business	5
Increase market share	24
Increase volume of Mexican operations	25
Increase lines of business	15
Reduce lines of business	2
Integrate operations into a U.S./North American network	15
Integrate operations into a global network	11
Reduce overheads of Mexican operations	10
Close Mexican operations	0

Source: North South Center study, 1994-1996.

None of the 37 respondents mentioned closing down Mexican operations as a goal, and only 5 said that their firms would seek to heighten the Mexican identity of the business, a critical change from a decade earlier, as in Canada.[104]

There are some interesting differences between the two sets of respondents. The most important of these deals with increasing lines of business. Few respondents at headquarters viewed increasing their firms' lines of business in Canada as a major near-term objective; more mentioned rationalizing lines of business as a likely outcome of integration. Canadian operations would cease to be "miniature replicas" of their parents, producing the whole range of the parents' products, and become instead more specialized in certain products or even components. In Mexico, however, fully 40 percent of the respondents — 14 of 37 — indicated that increasing lines of business was a key goal. And a somewhat larger share of headquarters respondents listed integrating Canadian operations into a U.S.-North

American or global production network than respondents in Mexico — although this difference may be due to the differing perceptions of headquarters and subsidiary managers.

Factors Driving Strategic and Structural Change in North America

The factors driving change in corporate strategy and structure in the 1990s differ fundamentally from those that influenced patterns of business in Canada and Mexico only a decade ago. As recently as the early 1980s, the organization and operations of U.S. firms in Canada and Mexico were substantially shaped by national regulations on such matters as local equity participation, "significant benefits," and technology transfer. Foreign firms still tended to view Canada and Mexico as distinct national markets, and most produced a wide range of their products in each country.

Today, national political and economic issues and regulatory requirements no longer exert such a powerful influence on corporate strategies and structures. This is particularly the case in manufacturing industries, although less so across the service sector. In Canada, Table 9 shows that headquarters executives, even though surveyed in the midst of one of Canada's most severe constitutional crises, still ranked this factor at the very bottom of the scale of those that drove change in their firms' corporate strategy and organization in North America.

Table 9.

**Factors Driving Change in Firm Strategy and Structure in North America
U.S. Headquarters Respondents**

(n=37)	Frequency of Rankings*					Total of Rankings	Average Ranking
	1	2	3	4	5		
Canada-U.S. FTA	4	5	7	13	5	112	3.29
Globalization	1	4	3	11	15	137	4.03
Canadian constitutional crisis	14	15	5	-	-	59	1.74
Canadian economic problems	10	7	12	5	-	80	2.35
International competition	-	4	5	15	10	133	3.91
Mexican growth potential	3	-	1	5	12	133	3.91
NAFTA	-	1	4	16	13	143	4.21
Product development/change	-	5	11	11	7	122	3.59
Changes in competitive advantage	2	-	11	14	7	126	3.71

* = Ratings are on a scale of 1 to 5, 1 being not very important; 3 being important; and 5 being very important. Total of Rankings is total score, and Average Ranking is the average rating on the 5-point scale.

Source: *U.S. Firms in North America: Redefining Structure and Strategy,* 1995 (Americas Society study).

Survey respondents saw the prospect of NAFTA — an economic community, not a trade agreement — as the most powerful driver of change (4.21 on a 5-point scale of importance). U.S. headquarters executives doubted that Canada's economic and constitutional crises would have much influence on their firms' future operations or organization, but they were more responsive to the potential impact of Mexican growth. Other highly ranked factors, including globalization, international competition, changes in competitive advantage, and "product development/change" are all dimensions of wider change in the business environment.

In the 1992 Conference Board of Canada survey, respondents gave greater weight to the impact of the recently implemented free trade agreement with the United States in driving the nature and pace of future rationalization. This confirms the conventional wisdom that Canada's commitment to the CUSFTA rested almost wholly upon the need to protect its trade and investment positions in the United States. However, when we assessed opinions at corporate headquarters only two years later, the CUSFTA was already old news. Executives at corporate headquarters almost universally viewed their firms' relationships with Canadian subsidiaries in terms of much wider interests and trends. Among these, NAFTA predominated, but NAFTA itself was seen, in our view, from a more global perspective.

This suggests that U.S. firms, at least at headquarters, assimilated the impact of the CUSFTA very rapidly. Changes in the relationship with their Canadian subsidiaries were undertaken in the context of wider changes in corporate organization and strategy. With rising international competition, tighter profit margins, and slow growth, the CUSFTA provided a clear and sound opportunity to reduce excess capacity while capturing continent-wide efficiency gains and to prepare these firms to engage international competitors in NAFTA as well as global markets.

It is important to recall that there are significant inter-industry differences. The findings in the Americas Society and North-South Center studies hold true for a wide range of industries in the manufacturing sector. But in some others, mainly in service sectors such as telecommunications, media, and financial services, the Canadian and Mexican governments have been more resistant, and patterns of liberalization and cross-border integration have been more complex. In these sectors, restrictions on foreign participation were more rigorous to begin with, and U.S. firms had traditionally occupied more tenuous positions. These industries, moreover, touch Canada's and Mexico's sensitive nerve of "identity" and cultural nationalism.

The results of our survey of Mexican subsidiaries parallel the findings of the earlier research. National issues and political and regulatory factors on such matters as local equity participation or technology transfer are no longer viewed by respondents at American subsidiaries in Mexico with the same weight as in the past. In addition, Mexico is no longer viewed as a distinct national market.

Table 10.

Factors Driving Change in Firm Strategy and Structure in North America: View from Mexican Subsidiaries

(n=37)	Frequency of Rankings*					Total of Rankings	Average Ranking
	1	2	3	4	5		
Canada-U.S. FTA	4	11	3	9	6	103	2.78
Globalization	0	1	8	9	17	151	4.08
Canadian developments	11	16	3	3	1	72	1.94
International competition	2	0	6	17	11	146	3.90
Mexican economic growth	0	1	5	11	20	166	4.48
Changes in Mexico	0	2	7	11	13	139	3.76
Prospects of NAFTA	0	2	5	16	14	158	4.27
Product development/change	1	4	15	9	6	125	3.38
Change in competitive advantage	0	4	3	18	8	133	3.60

* = Ratings are on a scale of 1 to 5, 1 being not very important; 3 being important; and 5 being very important.

Source: North South Center study, 1994-1996.

Mexico's economic short-term imbalances were not perceived by U.S. headquarters as reason for change in corporate strategies. Respondents continued to acknowledge Mexican economic growth as the major factor driving change in structure and strategies within a North American context (this factor received 4.48 on a 5-point scale). The prospective impact of NAFTA was the second most powerful driver of change. Other highly ranked factors were globalization and international competition. On the other hand, developments in Canada and the Canada-U.S. FTA were ranked as the least important.

Integration and Fears of Rationalization

During the debate in Canada leading up to the implementation of the Canada-U.S. Free Trade Agreement, Canadian politicians, economists, and other observers who opposed the deal predicted that, among other catastrophes, the agreement would ultimately cause a massive shake-out of manufacturing firms operating in Canada. According to this argument, those Canadian firms especially likely to cross the border to Buffalo and other U.S. sites would be Canadian subsidiaries of U.S.-based firms. With CUSFTA, these firms, which had been instrumental in helping Canada to achieve the world's highest standard of living, would have little reason to continue operations once tariff barriers had fallen. The fears heightened in the years immediately following the implementation of the CUSFTA. The recession of 1990-1991 severely strapped manufacturers as they tried to adjust to the new environment. Between 1990 and 1992, in a period of sharp recession, the number of Canadian manufacturing jobs shrank by 17 percent, and few observers were optimistic enough to suggest that those jobs were likely to return in the foreseeable future.

A study prepared for the Ontario Ministry of Industry, Trade and Technology was closer to the target, however, when it suggested that withdrawal was less likely than reorganization and rationalization:

> Two final points should be made: there is no major evidence that any company, whether favourably or unfavourably disposed, would close up shop in one country or the other on the basis of a Free Trade agreement. That is not to say that it would not happen, but when private companies have been asked by government officials what they would do, the first thought has been rationalization. That would lead one to believe that if a Free Trade agreement were reached, there would not be any massive closings of plants, but plant functions might be considerably altered as companies seek to make use of their new found flexibility.[105]

A widespread corporate pull-out from Canada did not take place. Only two of 31 respondents report that their firms had actually closed down their Canadian operations. More than this, three firms established new Canadian headquarters in this period. The same holds true for Mexico. None of the respondents there said that they had closed down Mexican operations.

While few U.S. subsidiaries in Canada closed down their operations, many were restructured and rationalized. In the earlier Conference Board survey, fully three-quarters of the respondents reported that their firms had recently undergone some type of rationalization. Asked to identify areas of rationalization that had occurred since 1989, respondents from Canadian subsidiaries answered that the scale of production was most likely to be rationalized, followed by rationalization in new product/new service opportunities and in marketing.

Table 11.

Areas of Significant Change Since 1989 Among Firms Reporting Rationalization — Subsidiaries of U.S.-based Parents Canadian Subsidiary Respondents

(n=31)

Area of Change	%
Scale of production	44
New production opportunities	35
Marketing	29
Degree of specialization/sophistication	27
Quality	24
Alternative supplies and services	21
Location	21
Changes to new suppliers	19
Upgrading inputs	18
Codes and standards	15

Source: *Multinational Firms Across the Canada-US Border: An Investigation of Intrafirm Trade and Other Activities,* 1992.

For many U.S. subsidiaries in Canada, rationalizing the scale of production meant a reduction in their manufacturing capacity. The Conference Board survey found few across-the-board plant closings, and this was not viewed by respondents as an immediate threat. Most respondents indicated that the reduction in manufacturing capacity was carried out selectively, particularly as subsidiary production operations were restructured to conform with new corporate strategies designed to meet the conditions of North American rather than just Canadian markets. In a period of widespread recession, liberalization of trade barriers, and heightened global competition, U.S. firms laid out new strategies to reduce excess capacity and to build integrated production networks across the U.S.-Canada border.

Canadian respondents to the Conference Board survey who cited rationalization in the scale of production tended to note that the number of production lines in Canada had been reduced, allowing (or forcing, as the case may be) subsidiaries to focus on a core product line. One company respondent noted, "Many operations were sold and closed to rationalize our manufacturing capacity and devote excess capacity to what is now the core business of our operation." Rationalization in the scale of production was carried out to help focus subsidiary attention on markets for its products, rather than on a specific geographic area, Canada, in which it had sole distribution rights. Many of these markets were in the United States, often other operations of its own firm; others were foreign. These findings show clearly that the traditional Canadian branch plant was dying, if not already dead. Another respondent in this survey observed, "Manufacturing has been restructured as part of a corporate strategic decision to rationalize production and focus on those global markets which hold the most promise."[106]

These responses match the findings of the Americas Society survey, in that downsizing of production capacity in Canada is part of a wider effort to define the Canadian operation's role within the firm on a continental and global basis. Put another way, the subsidiaries surveyed were attempting to find their place in what Robert Reich calls the parent firms' "global web of production."[107]

Warner-Lambert provides an interesting example of a firm that reduced the number of product lines manufactured in Canada in order to focus more on core products.

WARNER-LAMBERT

Late in 1992, Warner-Lambert decided to create Parke-Davis North America out of its Canadian, Mexican, and U.S. pharmaceutical operations. Reporting lines that flowed from the country manager to Parke-Davis in the United States were difficult and inefficient. As Parke-Davis products could be marketed in much the same manner in all three countries, the decision was made to centralize control for all of North America in one location.

CUSFTA and NAFTA had no great bearing on the decision. Instead, the perception of a North American market stretching across all three countries was the fundamental reason for the move. The move was also bolstered by Warner-Lambert's recent emphasis on developing global products.

In this new management, the Canadian and Mexican pharmaceutical units reported to the new president of Parke-Davis North America. The direct link between Parke-Davis in Canada and Warner-Lambert Canada was attenuated, creating a "host-tenant" relationship between the now separate but still affiliated division and Warner Lambert's Canadian headquarters.

These changes helped streamline the Parke-Davis operations and also raised important issues. The working relationship across the borders in North America helped Parke-Davis North America discover synergies hidden in the old system. While not every operation could be centralized, the company was able to see what operated best locally and where operations could be centralized. But there were challenges as well. Reconfiguring the relations among three distinct units has not been fully completed. Parke-Davis employees in Canada, Mexico, and the United States feared their positions were in jeopardy under a North American configuration because they were now parts of a larger, more complex organization. Downsizing was minimal in the organization worldwide, and there were no reductions in staff readily attributable to the creation of a Parke-Davis North America.

Mexicans seemed less fearful of significant downsizing, let alone a corporate pull-out, than Canadians. With a population nearly four times larger than Canada's, a much higher population growth rate, and increasing consumer demand, Mexican companies, including many U.S. subsidiaries as well as large domestic firms, anticipated that the overall impact of North American economic integration and market liberalization would lead to the expansion of business lines. Other favorable factors that shaped corporate attitudes were competitive wage rates, pressures to expand industrialization (particularly capital goods and access to technology), the development of local supplier relationships, and the seemingly unlimited U.S. demand for imports.

Downsizing operations in the scale of production and in new products, service, or marketing opportunities were, however, reported by several Mexican respondents. These developments typically have been a response to actual or expected increases in competition in the Mexican market following deregulation. For instance, as of 1995, Xerox had 60 percent of the market in Mexico and had enjoyed a 52-percent gross profit margin.[108] However, with tariff barriers dropping, competition with new entrants will be inevitable. Expected competition is forcing the company to rationalize its operations, basically dedicating more efforts to marketing and customer service.

United Airlines is another example of a company that is expecting more competition from more carriers from all three countries: U.S. Air, Alaska, American, Delta, Continental, and America West, along with smaller Mexican carriers. Mobil is also trying to boost its efficiency through economies of scale, given the expected absolute growth of the number of competitors. Texas Instruments is adopting a different strategy by trying to integrate small, and therefore more vulnerable, companies. These companies are being induced to become distributors rather than manufacturers, to fill market niches, to form joint venture partnerships, or to put themselves up for sale.

Reasons for Rationalization and Integration

In a 1995 article, journalist Greg Ip described changes in Black & Decker's strategy and operations in Canada:

> The Brockville [Ontario] operation hasn't always been used for export. Since arriving in town in 1957, Black & Decker's Canadian subsidiary, like other foreign-owned branch plants, had made small quantities of many products strictly for the Canadian market. But beginning in 1984, B&D's head office in Towson, Maryland, began to restructure worldwide. Operations in Canada were rationalized. B&D reduced the number of products made in Brockville, but the plant now makes them for the world markets. The overhaul has transformed the Brockville plant from a sheltered, Canadian company selling 80 percent of its products in Canada to a globally competitive, integral unit of North American operations exporting 65 percent of its output.[109]

Ip's description of Black & Decker parallels what firms in the study said about the efforts to rationalize and integrate their North American operations. First and by far most important, rationalization and integration are driven by the need to meet global competition. In an environment characterized by low growth, uncertain profit margins, and rapid technological change, competitive intensity soared. Dozens of companies that were household names for the better part of a century ceased to exist.

Reducing overcapacity is central to meeting competition. With technological change forcing the adoption of new forms of production and intensifying international competition, firms must shed excess production capacity if they are to survive in the new global economy. Protected by high tariff walls, many high-cost Canadian branch plants generated substantial profits for their corporate parents. Without protection and in an increasingly competitive environment, they are painful liabilities. As the Campbell Soup company's Annual Report stated in 1990: "We are closing high cost plants, carrying on a program begun last year. This restructuring will increase our capacity utilization, productivity, controls and quality. . . . The company's worldwide portfolio of business has been sharply refocused. Non-strategic and low-return businesses are being divested."[110] A respondent in a Canadian subsidiary commented in a similar fashion: "The current recession and greater competition have forced us to reassess our manufacturing capability, reduce costs, shrink production time and, most importantly, to improve the overall quality of our business."[111]

The Chairman and CEO of one the largest U.S. chemical firms observed in a similar fashion, "We are facing these new realities squarely. To operate profitably in today's conditions, we have cut our operating expenses, consolidated overlapping operations and made our organization more flexible and responsive." The aim is to create ". . . a more streamlined, horizontally integrated organization . . . that is geared to strengthen and accelerate implementation of global strategies."[112] One step in this direction was to combine the firm's North American core businesses into a single organization, with a good strategy and alignment of goals.

Asea Brown Boveri Ltd. (ABB), a Swiss-Swedish electrical engineering group, reorganized its global structure "to give business areas more responsibility when dealing with customers and to reduce overhead costs." A sluggish global economy and rising costs forced ABB to reorganize its "fragmented national managements into three economic regions: Europe, the Americas and Asia-Pacific." According to ABB CEO Percy Barnevik, "The opening-up of markets under the North American Free Trade Agreement made the establishment of one region for the Americas a logical step."[113]

Efforts to enhance quality in design, production, delivery, and service drive integration as well. With growing emphasis on customer satisfaction and total quality management, higher levels of integration are necessary to achieve greater control over quality and inventory. For instance, Revlon has been implementing the latest production techniques in its Mexican operations. Its strategy in Mexico is to provide quicker customer service, and this approach — rather than tariffs that were lowered before NAFTA — was the determining factor for the company's success.

Markets in North America are changing rapidly as well. Many have escaped entirely from national borders. Subsidiaries are becoming operations in Canada or Mexico rather than operations producing for Canada and Mexico. Distinct national markets have begun to blur, and branches with what once were national mandates now find themselves competing with other divisions in the firm. In this vein, another respondent in the North-South Center study told how his company is "finding more overlap in what we once thought of as separate customer bases."[114]

As firms restructure on a North American basis, others, suppliers for example, will do so as well. As the President of IBM Canada, William Etherington, observed, "As a response to the increasing number of customers that have been demanding cross-border services," our company intends to become "as seamless as possible across North America. If our customers are going to organize along North American lines, then our company will do the same."[115]

Markets can sometimes be serviced better by regional than by national sites. There is often no reason, it is observed, for a Quebec-based subsidiary of a U.S. firm to supply Canadian buyers in Vancouver. Firms are working out more rational, less expensive sourcing and marketing networks in North America. Xerox, for example, was beginning to ship products to Canadian customers directly from U.S. production sites in the early 1990s, rather than through a system of warehouses in Canada.[116]

Several cases provide important insights into why firms sought to rationalize and integrate their U.S., Canadian, and Mexican operations. Siemens AG, the German industrial group, decided to opt for a North American organization well before NAFTA was finally signed. It created a special task force charged with regionalizing production, with the object of cutting replication. At the end of 1993, a *Wall Street Journal* article reported, "All small-motor production is overseen by Siemen's Mexican operation, while large and medium-size motors are overseen by the U.S. unit. Cement-making equipment is controlled by Mexico, but engineering for steel is handled out of Atlanta. Shipbuilding equipment and some software operations belong to Canada. Some products, notably those controlled by things such as local building codes, will remain locally produced, but Siemens expects the vast majority of its production to be regional."[117]

The Dow Chemical Corporation is another example. Until 1991, Dow had no specific North American focus or unit specifically devoted to serving a North American market. During the last half of 1990 and early 1991, the company was active in developing joint ventures through its well established Canadian subsidiary to take advantage of opportunities generated by CUSFTA. More important, however, Dow's customers were already conducting business on a North American basis. As the president of Dow of Canada stated in 1992, "As a customer-driven company, we need to adapt to changes affecting our customers that are brought about by the globalization of the chemical industry, free trade and the escalating changes in the North American marketplace . . . . We really need a common approach to the increasing number of customers doing business on a North American basis."[118]

Faced with this new business reality of rising global competition, continuing margin pressures, and a lagging economy, Dow Chemical assembled a task team of senior managers from Dow Canada and Dow USA to identify opportunities in North America that would match Dow's core businesses. The team concluded, "A significant competitive advantage can be achieved by bringing together the two Areas with a common North American strategy. The new framework will mean one Area — Dow North America — with an overarching management structure built on the strengths of the two countries and single business teams for each of the core businesses. The core businesses will operate with a single strategy and scorecard for North America."[119]

Continental integration and rationalization will continue, expand, and intensify. For the North American multinational corporation, business policy responses will be based not on choice but on the necessity to survive and compete successfully in this dynamic new environment.

A Final Thought on Factors Driving Strategic and Structural Change in North America

Respondents in our surveys emphasized that political, regulatory, and even broad economic issues now play a much diminished role in corporate decisionmaking about strategy and structure. We do not doubt that this is true, at least insofar as certain key assumptions remain in place. One of the most fundamental of these is political stability. This is not something that troubled respondents to our surveys. But it would be unrealistic not to bear in mind that with regard to both Mexico and Canada, concerns about political stability have heightened in the past years. Mexico has pushed forward to further democratize its political system, but as one observer has mentioned recently, "The slowness and complexity of Mexico's transformation have generated extreme political and economic uncertainty."[120] In Canada, too, concerns about "national unity" — Quebec's role in the Confederation — have also intensified recently, and more Canadians than ever, it appears, believe that a major change in Canada's constitutional arrangements is all but inevitable, although this does not mean that Quebec will actually leave the Confederation.

In the corporate world, optimists still dominate thinking on both of these topics, and few companies are preparing to abandon either country because of political uncertainty. However, the elimination of traditional branch plants dedicated to national markets and the formation of continental networks, together with the continued existence of excess capacity in many industries, means that firms could relocate production fairly readily if they felt menaced by the prospect of political change. There appears to be no threat of this at the present time in Canada or Mexico, but continental integration does give firms much more flexibility to shift production within corporate networks.

Chapter Five

The Changing Experience of U.S. Subsidiaries in Canada and Mexico

The experiences of U.S. subsidiaries in Canada and Mexico have continued to change rapidly and substantially in the 1990s. Mexican and Canadian operations of U.S. firms are increasingly positioned as units within wider continental or global upstream and downstream corporate networks and are "as much a part of the whole skein of North American operations as a plant anywhere in the continental U.S," according to Canadian business researchers.[121] The aim of this chapter is to examine in more detail fundamental aspects of this changing relationship.

Intra-Firm Trade

Intra-firm relations are a critical dimension of the evolution of a North American economic space. Rising levels of intra-firm trade and the emergence of denser intra-firm production, sourcing, and marketing networks deepen the economic linkages among countries.

How is intra-firm trade likely to be affected by the evolving North American architecture? Respondents in the Americas Society and North-South Center surveys were asked how important intra-corporate trade with affiliates in Canada, Mexico, and the rest of the world would be in the next five years (see Tables 12 and 13).

Table 12.

Importance of Intra-firm Trade Over Next Five Years

U.S. Headquarters Respondents

(n=21)	Location of Affiliates		
	Canada	Mexico	Rest of the World
More Important	11	17	12
Less Important	1	0	0
About the Same	8	2	4
No Opinion	1	2	5

Source: *U.S. Firms in North America: Redefining Structure and Strategy, North American Outlook,* 1995 (Americas Society study).

Responses from U.S. headquarters respondents showed very high expectations that intra-firm trade would increase in North America and globally from 1994 through 1999. Even with intra-firm trade between the United States and Canada already at high levels, the majority of respondents forecast substantial increases. With regard to Mexico, their expectations were higher still.

The 1992 Conference Board of Canada survey of Canadian subsidiaries supported these conclusions but introduced other concerns. Forty-two percent of the Canadian respondents thought that imports from U.S. affiliates would increase over the next three years. The Canadian respondents underscored a variety of exogenous variables in accounting for increases in intra-firm trade. For example, some thought that optimism regarding an impending economic recovery would fuel expectations that an upward turn in the business cycle would increase demand for imports from affiliated suppliers in the United States. Other respondents in 1992 pointed to the impact of the exchange rate of the Canadian dollar on intra-firm trade. "Business is bad in all of North America," one said, "but our lower-cost U.S. affiliates are in direct competition now for a market which we traditionally held. The lowering of duties has helped our affiliates in the United States."[122]

Most Canadian subsidiary managers felt that rationalization in production capacity in Canada would lead to higher levels of intra-firm trade. As one respondent reported, "Our reorganization plan specifically indicates that an increase of affiliated imports will be necessary due to the scaling back of production at our Canadian sites."[123]

Respondents to the North-South Center survey also expected intra-firm trade with affiliates in North America and throughout the rest of the world to increase sharply over the next five years (1995-2000). These views conformed with a survey of U.S. companies in Mexico, conducted by the American Chamber of Commerce of Mexico in 1994, which found that managers in U.S. firms operating in Mexico felt that NAFTA would lead their companies to increase use of U.S. suppliers and to choose U.S. over other foreign suppliers.[124] Unlike the Canadian and headquarters respondents, these projections rested on expectations of economic growth in Mexico rather than on a major relocation of production.

Table 13.
Importance of Intra-Firm Trade over the Next Five Years
Mexican Subsidiary Respondents

(n=36)	Location of Affiliates		
	Mexico	Canada	Rest of the World
More Important	30	12	20
Less Important	2	0	1
About the Same	3	9	17
No Opinion	1	2	2

Source: North-South Center study, 1994-1996.

Respondent views about rising levels of intra-firm trade were laced at times with a sharp dash of skepticism regarding how this would affect their own operations. Some Canadian subsidiary managers felt that their U.S. parent was actively reconsidering the need to manufacture in Canada. They felt that, as product lines were scaled back in Canada, subsidiaries would begin to assume the role of distributor of many of the products once produced in Canada. One senior executive commented, "Imports from the United States have increased as production facilities in Canada have contracted. It is ironic that we're selling goods from our U.S. parent that we were making just two years ago."[125]

Similar views were expressed by several Mexican respondents. Kodak, for example, is anticipating stronger intra-firm competition, given acute excess capacity. This is creating a serious problem that is expected to be addressed through more communication and technical support between branches and subsidiaries. Singer's regional controller pointed out, "Intra-firm trade is a double-edged sword. Intra-company purchases from Asia, particularly mainland China, allow us to compete effectively with low cost/high quality products — even with a 20 percent import duty. At the same time, there's lots of bottom line pressure, with U.S.-made Singer products competing head-on against Singer Mexicana."[126]

Some Mexican respondents, like their Canadian colleagues, fear that trimming product lines would force subsidiaries to play a larger role in distribution. In varying degrees, Revlon, Singer, and Black and Decker have all increased and broadened their distribution in Mexico of products from their firms' global affiliates.

SARA LEE

Sara Lee, a U.S.-based producer of personal and household products and foods, fueled its expansion drive through the acquisition of a number of local companies. In 1991 and 1992, Sara Lee acquired Rinbros, Mexico's leading manufacturer of men's and boys' underwear; Mallorca, the country's second largest hosiery manufacturer; and Estelar, a smaller pantyhose maker. It also acquired the multinational Playtex, Mexico's largest manufacturer of bras. All of these acquisitions complemented the establishment of a Mexican subsidiary of Hanes, a hosiery and underclothes manufacturer owned by Sara Lee. The relationship between Hanes and Rinbros was one of independence in marketing and brand identity but consolidation in sourcing, production, and distribution resources. For example, Rinbros' inputs were sourced through the Hanes Knit Products network, and some Hanes products were manufactured in Rinbros plants.

Sara Lee preferred to keep local management intact when it brought other companies into its fold. Since it is a marketing-oriented company, Sara Lee's management opted to keep the decision-making process decentralized in order to provide flexibility in day-to-day decisions. It chose 100 percent ownership over part ownership and joint ventures, to keep decisionmaking speedy. It poured investment into new acquisitions to increase production capacity, and it encouraged communications across its diverse Mexican properties.[127]

Among multinational corporations, competitive tensions may grow as headquarters' global strategic objectives conflict with their subsidiaries' market plans and strategies. Pressure on consolidated balance sheets may lead parent firms to scale back or even phase out subsidiary activities in, for example, the manufacture of certain goods or the provision of services in favor of local acquisitions or intra-firm sourcing. Just as in the case of the U.S. machine tool industry in the 1980s, manufacturers may find themselves transformed into distributors by market pressure and the need to maintain overall profitability.

The picture that emerges from these data is varied and complex. Executives at U.S. headquarters tended to focus more on the integration of Canadian, U.S., and Mexican affiliates into a North American system. Canadian executives were more likely to be concerned with possible losses in production capacity and jobs, as higher levels of integration and intra-firm trade would force downsizings and rationalization in a fairly mature market. Mexican managers have tended to be more optimistic because they viewed Mexico as a rapidly expanding market and were more likely to see increased intra-firm trade as a source of cost reductions and, therefore, a vehicle for expansion. All were aware, however, that decisions regarding organization and strategy were not being made in a vacuum but rather in the midst of economic and political uncertainty.

Still, none of this suggested a zero-sum game in which intra-firm trade within one segment of a firm (U.S.-Mexico) was replacing that of another segment (U.S.-Canada). Respondents projected a more rapid growth of intra-firm trade with Mexico but did not suggest that trade with Canadian subsidiaries would collapse. The major force here was expectation of rapid economic growth in Mexico rather than the massive relocation of production. For Canadians, the challenge was seen to reside in redefining the role of their operations within the corporate network.

Strategic Alliances

Strategic alliances are becoming critical elements in corporate relationships, and corporate business strategies rely increasingly on alliances as links among Mexico, the United States, and Canada deepen. Strategic alliances have become particularly important in Mexico. In the past, foreign companies in Mexico were forced to form joint ventures because Mexican law limited them to minority stakes. Since regulations were liberalized, however, alliances have been relied upon for other purposes. Globalization of the marketplace, rising R&D costs, and the need to establish a foothold in a rapidly growing market explain why companies take this route in the 1990s.[128]

Some U.S. consumer goods companies have formed distribution alliances with Mexico-based consumer goods companies. Scott Paper's Mexico subsidiary, Crisoba Products Consumidor, has eased the way for newcomers to enter the market. In 1990, Crisoba entered into an arrangement with First Brands of Danbury, Connecticut, to distribute Glad sandwich and garbage bags. The companies also shared advertising and consulted on marketing. In this way, First Brands gained access to a first-class distribution network without a large investment. As a result, the alliance was stronger than a straight producer-distributor contract.

Mazda

In one of the most successful joint ventures in Mexico to date, Ford and Mazda worked together during the 1980s to establish Ford's new $500 million automobile stamping and assembly plant in Hermosillo, Mexico. The undertaking included a large-scale transfer of technology from Mazda to Ford that included project design, tooling and equipment, a quality system, and assistance in employee training. Training Hermosillo's workers in Japanese management methods took place in five countries on three continents. Ford considered the Hermosillo project an ideal laboratory to try this sort of training, as union policies in the United States made it difficult to institute new training and quality systems at home. The auto giant hoped that a successful experience in Mexico would have a favorable influence on future contracts with the United Auto Workers in the United States and Canada.

Besides the profitable prospects of selling kits and parts to Ford for assembly in Mexico and earning fees from Ford for technology and technical support, Mazda's management, initially unenthusiastic about Ford's proposed project, developed an interest in the venture because it fit into Mazda's long-term goal of internationalizing its operations: Mazda viewed the project as an opportunity to learn more about Ford's cost-control practices and the process of launching a major manufacturing facility in a foreign country.

Outstanding quality and productivity results were achieved at Hermosillo. Success led Ford to use the Mexican plant as a prototype in restructuring the operations of its plant in Wayne, Michigan. The Wayne plant was converted and retooled to incorporate some of the advanced technology and organization, production, and quality concepts used at Hermosillo. Moreover, because of its quality and productivity achievements at Hermosillo, Ford was able to negotiate a new contract successfully with the United Auto Workers that embodied these efficiency gains.[129]

Autonomy

Our surveys of U.S. headquarters executives and of managers in U.S. subsidiaries in Mexico, together with materials from the 1992 Conference Board of Canada survey, shed light on changing patterns of autonomy of U.S. subsidiaries operating in Canada and Mexico. Autonomy has been a critical issue for Canadians working in subsidiaries of U.S. firms. Canadian concerns increased in many cases, as might be expected, with deeper economic integration. In the case of Mexico, the starting point was different and the level of concern about diminished autonomy substantially less.

The Americas Society and North-South Center survey research teams asked respondents at U.S. headquarters and in Mexican subsidiaries to compare present (1994) levels of autonomy in various corporate functions with the situation in 1988. We learned that while levels of intra-firm integration and coordination with parent firms were higher in 1994 than a few years earlier, the creation of new organizational structures had not meant that local autonomy had diminished in every function.

Headquarters respondents, for the most part, said that their Canadian operations had retained since 1988 much the same level of autonomy in most functions. Two-thirds or more of the respondents said that local autonomy in 1994 was the same or greater than 1988 in nine out of 13 functions polled; in four functions, approximately 10 percent of the respondents said that local autonomy was less in 1994 than 1988 (Table 14).

Table 14.

Changes in Autonomy of Canadian Operations

U.S. Headquarters Respondents

(n=33)	Degree of Autonomy in 1994 Compared to 1988		
Corporate Function	Same	Less	More
Treasury	24	7	2
Finance	23	8	2
Investment (including M&A)	21	10	2
Production Planning	19	12	2
Sales	26	5	3
Procurement	25	6	2
Advertising	22	6	4
Research	19	12	2
Development	22	10	1
Exporting	23	8	1
Management Appointment	22	8	3
Marketing Research	25	5	3
Public Affairs	25	5	3

Source: *U.S. Firms in North America: Redefining Structure and Strategy, North American Outlook,* 1995 (Americas Society study).

This was the view from U.S. headquarters of the firms polled. Another study, conducted by The Conference Board of Canada in 1994, focused on the managers of Canadian subsidiaries. It found that 58 percent of the firms that participated in their survey (Japanese, European, and U.S.) had seen no change in the relationship with their parents over the previous five years.[130] Of those respondents who reported a major change in the relationship with their parent, two-thirds reported a weakening of the subsidiary head office's role, and 58 percent said that direct reporting lines to the parent had been strengthened. Thirty percent saw the role of the subsidiary head office strengthened. Deeper integration was particularly evident in high-tech industries. Almost three-quarters of firms in high technology sectors reported that headquarters control had increased. With regard to U.S. firms, 81 percent reported that the decision-making power of their Canadian offices had been weakened, and 63 percent said that reporting lines to divisions or operating companies had been strengthened.

These data create a fairly coherent picture. The majority of respondents in several surveys reported that the operating autonomy of Canadian subsidiaries remained at approximately the same level as in the past. Some firms reported that the autonomy of their Canadian operations had increased in this period of integration, particularly with regard to sales, advertising, and market research, where localization has most value. A fairly large number of firms reported that Canadian operations had less autonomy with regard to investment, production planning, and research and development. Where changes were reported, the trend since 1988 has been toward diminishing autonomy, particularly in functions relating to product development. This was particularly true in high-tech manufacturing.

These findings support the view that new continental and global relationships necessitate closer coordination of efforts, particularly in those sectors that have felt the greatest pressure of global competition, such as high-tech production where firms have had to rationalize operations and utilize the latest technology simply to remain in the market. While some subsidiaries have been left to fend for themselves, the more common experience is one of tightening business linkages within the firm. To survive, the subsidiary must be able to fit into the structure and activities of the firm by fulfilling a role in the firm's overall strategy.

A closer reading of this data, together with interviews with respondents, suggest more complex changes in autonomy and reporting relationships. The weakening of subsidiary head office authority is frequently linked, not with the strengthening of corporate parent headquarters authority, but rather with stronger operating companies or business units. Some of these are North American and some are U.S. units. In this situation, the role of the parent headquarters also has often decreased, as firms have decentralized to their operating companies or strategic business units. This is particularly the case in high-tech firms like Hewlett Packard, where operating units in Canada and the United States report directly to global, North American, or U.S. units — and where reporting lines to HP Canada are "dotted line."

The resulting shift in the balance of responsibilities troubles some senior executives in Canadian subsidiaries: "There's a lot of anxiety now among the CEOs of some subsidiaries. There's less empowerment, less freedom to exercise initiative. Canadian CEOs are concerned with domestic issues such as regulatory requirements, labor law and human rights. But in terms of really hard issues, such as long-term planning, the parent companies are pulling back."[131] Other Canadian managers seem more comfortable with their changing roles within the corporate system. Cooperation between subsidiaries and headquarters seems to have increased on technical matters and with regard to customers. A manager in a Canadian subsidiary says his company is taking a team approach to integration with its parent company and affiliates in the United States: "In cooperation with our parent company, there are now North American business and marketing teams with joint Canada-U.S. participation as part of the strategic plan."[132]

IBM[133]

IBM began a large-scale reorganization and downsizing of its highly centralized global organization late in 1990. The aim was to achieve a balance between centralization and decentralization to improve IBM's ability to meet customer needs and create a competitive cost structure.

First, IBM centralized many business units and functions in order to "identify and reduce duplication of effort between the current organizations, enabling IBM to have a more competitive cost structure." National business units — IBM Canada, IBM USA, IBM Taiwan, and IBM Germany — were consolidated into regional entities such as IBM North America, IBM Asia-Pacific, and IBM Europe.

In North America, the Canadian marketing and sales group was integrated with the U.S. parent, the first step in the creation of a North American Division. "As a response to the increasing number of customers that have been demanding cross-border services," IBM will become "as seamless as possible across North America. . . . If your customers are organized on a North American basis, we have to organize on a North American basis too."

Sales and marketing responsibilities were transferred to a regional division; however, the Canadian unit maintained its autonomy in other functional areas. A senior executive in the Canadian operation observed, "There is no reason to think that the [Canadian] company will not win mandates to manage certain categories of business within the North American set-up." The director of Canadian operations will have "full discretion to make decisions to keep the Canadian operations profitable."

As a second step, management decentralized many functions and created autonomous divisions to become more mobile, entrepreneurial, and market-oriented: "[We are] redefining IBM from a single centralized company into a network of more competitive businesses. . . . Each will be fast and focused on the markets it chooses to serve."[134]

Decentralization is a logical strategy. John Akers, former chairman of the board, stated, "Putting a premium on autonomy will unleash the full creativity of our people to achieve greater speed, agility and ingenuity in delivering the right products, services and solutions."[135]

IBM Canada is in the process of "spinning off two units in a bid to win a larger piece of the computer network services market. The two divisions will form one new company . . . [and] remain a wholly owned subsidiary of IBM Canada."[136]

IBM's objective is to create a structure and strategy that is capable of adapting to the changes in the business environment and balancing the levels of autonomy in the business.

Mexican responses with regard to the issue of autonomy revealed a different trajectory from Canadian responses, but both were headed in the same direction. U.S. subsidiaries in Mexico, such as the Mexican affiliate of Texas Instruments, were often quite independent of headquarters in the past. With an increasingly North American vision, they are becoming even less closely linked to corporate headquarters and are more likely to report to operating units. Many factories in Mexico, for example, reported directly to operating units of their parent companies.

Mexican managers in these operations often had a different perspective on these developments from Canadian managers. Mexican respondents generally felt that North American trade and investment integration were likely to lead to more production and more opportunities for both domestic and international sales. Table 15 shows that respondents at U.S. subsidiaries in Mexico were more likely to feel that their operations have either retained the same levels of autonomy or have increased their independence in most functions since 1988.

Table 15.
Changes in Autonomy of Mexican Operations
Mexican Subsidiary Respondents

(n=34)	Degree of Autonomy in 1995 Compared to 1988		
Corporate Function	Same	Less	More
Treasury	19	4	11
Finance	15	3	7
Investment (including M&A)	14	7	11
Production Planning	12	5	14
Sales	15	2	16
Procurement	17	4	16
Advertising	15	4	13
Research	14	6	9
Development	11	7	9
Exporting	15	3	11
Management Appointment	15	1	17
Marketing Research	18	2	16
Public Affairs	18	0	13

Source: North-South Center study, 1994-1996.

About half of the Mexican subsidiary respondents reported increased autonomy with regard to management appointments, sales, procurement, and marketing research. Production planning and advertising were mentioned 14 and 13 times, respectively. Mexican subsidiaries reported diminished autonomy in product development and investment, areas in which decisions are more likely to be executed at business unit level or at company headquarters.

What accounts for these differences between how managers of Canadian and Mexican subsidiaries view changing patterns of autonomy? Canadians seem to be more fearful of integration because the volume of trade and interaction between Canada and the United States is so huge and the patterns of business behavior so similar with those of the United States that they could be easily overwhelmed. They fear that their operations will lose a distinct identity and role within the firm. If levels of U.S.-Canada integration in many firms were so high even before CUSFTA that the continued existence of Canadian subsidiaries was threatened, Mexican subsidiaries began with a much greater sense of distance from their corporation headquarters. U.S. firms traditionally assigned much lower weight to their subsidiaries in the less developed countries, including Mexico. This sense of distance between corporate headquarters in the United States and their operations in Mexico has been intensified by the deep cultural differences between the Anglo North and the Latin South. Differences in historical, cultural, political, legal, economic, and commercial environments between the United States and Mexico have greatly influenced the goals, objectives, plans, structures, strategies, and activities of U.S. firms in Mexico.

Cultural factors shape sales, marketing, and service activities in Mexico. A product's design, function, packaging, marketing, promotion, advertising, sales, and after-purchase service are all markedly influenced by cultural factors. As one example, Black & Decker's head of Mexican operations pointed out, "The electric blender is the food processor of Latin America. Whether for making shakes, pureeing vegetables or liquefying sauces, the blender is the all purpose appliance; consequently, it requires a motor that is much stronger than that manufactured for use in the U.S. where the blender is no substitute for a food processor and other kitchen appliances and gadgets."[137]

Responses to North American Integration

Corporate cultures, management style, and the sensitivity of people involved all shape new organizational arrangements that integrate formerly distinct national systems and determine levels of autonomy for different units of a firm. As the Dow Chemical Company was establishing a new North American business division, its leadership was aware of the pitfalls that might hinder this process. A task team set up by Dow Canada and Dow USA warned of barriers to the implementation of this plan. First were "people issues," such as the development of cross-border teams and reporting relationships, which would have to be managed effectively. Second, maintaining high levels of customer service and satisfaction through the transition would be a serious challenge. Third, "common scorecards" for core business performance would have to be developed.[138]

In this case, it was assumed that while the Canadian company president would continue to oversee operations in Canada, the nature of his tasks and the role of the Canadian operations were likely to change significantly. In its response to the Americas Society questionnaire, managers at Dow headquarters said that the Canadian operations would probably have less autonomy over R&D, marketing and public affairs, but would gain more authority over product development and sales. Making these changes, they said, would not be easy.[139]

Canadian managers in a number of companies voice strong opinions about the impact of these changes in structure and strategy. Some acknowledge that Canadian branch plants have lacked much input into the corporate mainstream. The head of the subsidiary of a U.S. chemical firm observed, "We were viewed by our customers, by the government and even by our parent company as not adding a lot of value. We were just selling products."[140]

Other Canadian managers charge that it is more difficult to stay ahead of global competitors or to service local needs locally when key strategic functions have been removed. A vice president of a major U.S. chemical company's Canadian subsidiary states, " . . . in principle . . . the strategic direction for my business must be set at headquarters, with a global focus . . . . However, . . . strategies have to be adapted to local circumstances."[141] Canadians observe that globalization is not equivalent to Americanization, and integration is more acceptable to Canadian executives in a continental or global system than when Canadian business operations are collapsed into U.S. strategic business units.

U.S. heavy-handedness is never appreciated, and another generation of Canadian managers in U.S. subsidiaries stamp their feet in frustration, for example, "I would like to see the U.S. managers in direct-connect businesses listen to what we have to say rather than assuming their methods for doing business are always right. Contrary to what they may think, Americans can learn from Canadians."[142]

Authority and responsibility have not only flowed back to corporate headquarters. Several major firms have created new cross-border regions that are organized around Canadian-based operations. Digital Equipment of Canada is responsible for the company's computer systems unit in 11 central U.S. states, and Microsoft Canada is responsible for sales, consulting, and systems engineering in an 18-state U.S. region.[143] These examples remain exceptions, however, and Canadian managers still agree that the size of their U.S. parent companies, a lack of sensitivity to Canadian concerns, and a prevailing tendency to approach global issues from a domestic perspective can make U.S. executives at headquarters difficult associates.

Increased intrafirm competition puts new pressures on Canadian managers. Subsidiaries recognize that they will be under increasing scrutiny to achieve the business goals set by headquarters or division management. Local managers know that they will be under constant pressure to reduce costs and improve profits. Leaner, more integrated Canadian operations will provide fewer opportunities for Canadian managers, and more downsizing is likely.

Rationalization has not affected Canadian subsidiaries alone, however. U.S. headquarters personnel have been cut drastically in most firms, and downsizing has taken place in plants throughout the United States. It simply is not true, as Canadian journalists occasionally infer, that a job lost in Canada is a job saved in the United States.

Ownership Patterns

Some evidence suggests that ownership patterns are shifting as well. Although some Canadians felt it was a waste of local capital to purchase shares of U.S. subsidiaries already located in Canada, wider Canadian equity participation was a key element in "good Canadian corporate citizenship" in the 1970s. That trend has been weakened if not reversed in the 1990s, and various Canadian subsidiaries have reported that they have been bought out by their U.S. parents.[144] GE, for example, in 1989 purchased the minority of its Canadian operation that had been held by Canadians. This helped put in place GE's "direct connect" system, in which Canadian business units report directly to U.S. Strategic Business Units rather than to the head of Canadian General Electric. In the 1994 Conference Board survey, about 16 percent of the responding firms reported that Canadian ownership in their businesses had decreased; of these firms, three-quarters were bought out by the parent company.

It is not clear, however, whether these changes in ownership should be viewed purely in terms of the relationship between U.S. parent companies and their Canadian subsidiaries. Stock buybacks for financial and governance purposes were undertaken widely during the past decade, not only of subsidiaries but of U.S. parent corporations as well. Buyouts of Canadian subsidiaries may be less a function of efforts to diminish Canadian autonomy than a dimension of wider changes in financial structure and corporate governance.

Parent-subsidiary relationships are also affected by a nation's culture and political economy. The changing nature of the North American market and the more liberal regulatory environment in Mexico have influenced the ownership patterns of subsidiaries there. Ralston Purina, the U.S. pet food producer, reacquired nearly 100 percent of the shares in its Mexican subsidiary that had been delisted in 1990. Previously, when the 1973 Foreign Investment Law limited foreign ownership to 49 percent, the firm had sold off its majority interest to Mexican investors. Regaining ownership permitted the company to embark on a strategy that fit the Mexican operation into the company's global strategy. Expanding its operations and boosting quality to take on a more competitive environment, Ralston Purina also standardized brands, packaging, and ingredients. The products sold in Mexico, therefore, were the same as those sold in the United States and in some other countries. Ralston Purina adjusted production in Mexico: some products were phased out, some were imported from the United States, and some product lines were kept in Mexico to take advantage of lower costs.[145]

Intra-Firm Competition for Mandates

When Canadian, Mexican, and U.S. managers talk about corporate organization in this era of strategic and structural change, they seem to have several different models in mind. One model focuses more on efforts to capture efficiencies and synergies globally through tightly centralized control of key activities. As Professors Allen Morrison and Kendall Roth observe, "To achieve maximum synergies as well as economies of scale, the actions of subsidiaries are tightly linked or integrated across countries. As a result, subsidiaries perform only those activities that leverage location-specific advantages or in which the subsidiary has a distinctive capability to perform."[146] Subsidiaries are forced to focus on a single dimension of the business, determined by their specific competitive advantages.

An alternative model envisages a different dynamic at the core of global organizational change. Instead of being driven by centralized efforts to capture efficiencies by allocating functions, subsidiaries are driven by competition among themselves for mandates to carry out whatever activities each feels it can handle. In this model, the dynamic is less centralized allocation by corporate headquarters than entrepreneurial competition among operations in a more decentralized and networked firm.

Both of these are ideal types rather than models of actual organizations. Neither is likely to appear in a pure form; in reality it will be found in some combination of the two. However, it is interesting to see, as we review comments and literature on the subject, that subsidiary managers who are more pessimistic about the future have a negative view of the centralized model. They cite the dangers inherent in centralization at U.S. headquarters and the consequent loss of autonomy and relevance of the subsidiary within the organization. Those managers with a more optimistic view of the future concur that centralization has many drawbacks and focus, instead, on the entrepreneurial possibilities for subsidiaries through competing for mandates within the firm, as described in the second model.

One participant in the 1992 Conference Board survey of Canadian subsidiaries put himself in the seat of the CEO of his U.S. parent and asked, "Why do I need to have a plant in Canada if I can manufacture more cheaply in the United States and supply Canada without duties to worry about?"[147] The answer, of course, is that fewer and fewer firms will think about "supplying Canada" as a distinct and separate national market. Each operation in Canada, no less than any other plant, must now compete aggressively for development, production, and marketing mandates.

The success of Honeywell Canada in winning mandates, for example, has rested on its "proven ability to design, develop and manufacture competitive, quality products for exports to global markets, according to its vice president and general manager."[148] Is economic integration viewed as an opportunity or a risk? A Canadian manager in a U.S. subsidiary argued that CUSFTA was a key opportunity, despite pressures it would generate to reduce his firm's product lines. "It will allow us to focus on products we make exceptionally well, and it will allow us to drop products we make mainly to avoid paying border tariffs. And it will give us opportunities to provide new products to U.S. customers at competitive prices."[149]

The Americas Society survey of U.S. headquarters executives shows that they anticipated a substantial increase of intra-firm competition for mandates. Respondents were asked in 1994 whether the level of intra-firm competition for mandates had increased or decreased in the past five years. Table 16 shows that respondents saw internal competition for product mandates as being on the rise.

Table 16.

As compared to five years ago [1989-1990], which section below best describes the current level of competition for product lines and/or mandates among your firm's global network of subsidiaries and affiliates?

U.S. Headquarters Respondents

(n=21)	No. of Firms	%
Competition has increased greatly	9	42.9
Competition has increased slightly	4	19.0
Competition has stayed about the same	3	14.3
Competition has decreased	0	-
No competition for product lines/mandates	3	14.3
No opinion	2	9.5

Source: *U.S. Firms in North America: Redefining Structure and Strategy,* 1995 (Americas Society study).

Almost half of the U.S. headquarters managers said that competition for product mandates or lines among their firms' global network of subsidiaries had increased greatly in the past five years. This supports the view that internal production markets are as sensitive to globalization as external markets.

Professors Morrison and Roth's 1993 survey of 124 subsidiaries of multinational corporations shows that the problems of strategic adjustment facing Canada are scarcely unique. Their examination suggests that subsidiaries are not necessarily victims in the program of reorganization. Instead, they found that "subsidiaries typically have considerable control over their fortunes, and that they can do much to develop the characteristics that lead to greater autonomy through global subsidiary mandates." The key to the development of mandates, they find, is that "managerial competence and manufacturing skills are far more important than both strong export sales and marketing skills."[150]

As traditional product lines have been scaled back, Canadian and Mexican subsidiaries are being spurred to develop new products that can be marketed worldwide. One Canadian respondent noted, "New products are going to be the key to our future growth, and we have started to spend more time promoting our products outside of Canada."[151] Another Canadian manager in a U.S. subsidiary described how his firm was seeking to find or develop new products and then market them effectively, "We are trying to improve our ability to use and develop new technologies and our marketing management capabilities to be competitive in global markets."[152] A third executive in a Canadian subsidiary summed up the situation in these terms, "The most significant change has been in marketing where we have focused on improving our ability to sell our products anywhere in the world."[153]

Addressing this shift in approach, an executive in a Canadian subsidiary agreed that the most difficult transition would be to get out of the "Canada only" mindset to capitalize on opportunities in other markets. He commented that for as long as he had been with the firm, Canadian management found a convenient excuse in the policies of their parent company for not marketing more aggressively in the United States. Now, since the CUSFTA, there would no longer be room for excuses.[154]

The CEO of a Canadian subsidiary lamented the passing of "the golden age of the country management." The very existence of country managers would become suspect, he said, unless they could substantiate and justify the unique skills their subsidiaries possessed.[155] This is surely true, but not only for country management. It applies equally to the management of every operation within a firm. Intra-firm competition for production mandates is much tougher than ever before, and business unit managers in any part of the firm — not just in Canada or Mexico — know they will be constantly forced to justify their existence in the eyes of their parent.

The bottom line is the collapse of protected, import-substitution economies and the need to build globally competitive North American businesses. The CEO of the Canadian subsidiary of a major U.S. consumer-goods products manufacturer observed, "Canada has no choice. We either win big and have big factories that supply at least North America, if not the world, or we're not going to have any factories at all."[156]

Canadian managers have worried that their operations would suffer from significant competitive disadvantages in this new intra-firm competition. Most important, competition was increasing for the Canadian markets upon which they long relied, as other operations of their own firms sought to expand their mandates. Many thought that input costs, especially labor and some supplies, would probably remain higher for Canadian firms than for many of their competitors, including U.S. companies. Additionally, Canada's climate for business was criticized by many Canadian managers. Labor legislation and environmental standards are perceived as threats to the ability of U.S. subsidiaries to continue producing in Canada.

Others believe that Canada provides substantial competitive advantages that will actually attract more investment and new operations. The Canadian government's Department of Foreign Affairs and International Trade and the former Investment Canada organized a series of roundtable discussions with the CEOs and other senior managers of Canadian subsidiaries of multinational corporations in 1993 and 1994. Many of the corporate participants' comments parallel our findings. The quality of the Canadian workforce and the high-tech capacity of Canadian-based operations were often mentioned. For example, in a lighting fixture and controls company, a particular product was identified as "an area where we saw potential for significant growth. The product line is very technically complex and at the time of the pitch did not represent significant production for the larger US facilities. Our goal is to do a major re-design on this product offering in an effort to reduce costs . . . and to win the mandate and service the entire North American market."[157] Reflecting Canada's international experience and expertise, the president of Hughes Aircraft of Canada said, "Canada is viewed as an international trading country with a knowledge-based economy." Hughes' expansion in Canada has been a result of Canada's advanced activity and competence in high tech, particularly in air traffic control.[158] Other assets are government support for research and development and government export financing. Participants underlined Canadian tax incentives and access to foreign markets. They called attention to Canada's legal environment, characterized by less litigation than in the United States. Finally, the quality of life in Canada, compared to that in the United States, was attractive to many executives and their families.

The Black and Decker story follows this line. Strategic change, directed toward a new North American focus, drove organizational change as well. B&D plants, sales, and marketing units now report to their corresponding chiefs in Maryland. Business journalist Greg Ip wrote in 1995 that corporate culture at B&D Canada had changed, too:

> 'We didn't have the same focus when we were just a Canadian company,' according to Bob Larocque, site director for the plant. 'What's important is we have to be focused on being competitive in North America. Through the late '80s, I had a lot of discussions with employees who said we can't be competitive with the U.S., their standard of living, their costs and their labor rates are lower. [I said] that's true, but at the end of day, if we're not competitive, we won't be working.'[159]

Ip reported in the same article that B&D's transformation from an inward-looking manufacturer into a North American company helped insulate the Brockville plant from the severity of Canada's recession and that, as of 1995, the company had done so well that it not only avoided layoffs but had almost doubled its sales since 1992.

Mexican experiences show as well that a major driver of change in corporate organization is competition among subsidiaries for mandates. More than half of the Mexican subsidiary respondents to the North-South Center survey said that competition among their firms' global network of subsidiaries had increased significantly in the past five years.

In the case of Black and Decker, intra-firm competition is having a negative impact on Mexican operations, particularly since the cost of doing business is high (due to poor infrastructure and services, governmental regulation, and high labor costs). As one executive claimed, "Black and Decker Mexico's main competitor is Black and Decker USA. NAFTA brought certainty and with it transborder shipments that are hurting us. We previously enjoyed a protected market locally, but thanks to NAFTA we have benefited, nevertheless, by being forced to become more competitive — our output has tripled. With trade liberalization markets open throughout the Americas, competitive pressure will increase: we expect to source from and sell into many different markets to stay ahead."[160]

For Kodak, intra-firm competition is a reality, due to incessant changes in business lines, organizational structures, and operations — not to mention the dire need for operations in mature markets such as the United States to reverse declining sales revenues by exporting to growing markets, even at the expense of local subsidiaries. "With excess capacity all over there, the pressure to meet competition both from within and from outside is intense. We must continually boost service quality, improve communications within the firm's network, and strengthen technical support."[161]

Table 17.

As compared to five years ago [in 1989-1990], which sector below best describes the current level of competition for product lines and/or mandates among your firm's global network of subsidiaries and affiliates?

Mexican Subsidiary Respondents

(n=37)	No. of Firms	%
Competition has increased greatly.	21	56.8
Competition has increased slightly.	7	19.0
Competition has stayed about the same.	0	0.0
Competition has decreased.	1	2.8
No competition for product lines/mandates	7	19.0
No opinion	1	2.8

Source: North-South Center study, 1994-1996.

In the past, subsidiaries of U.S. multinational firms in Mexico and Canada focused their attention mainly on protected national markets. Today, these operations increasingly participate in wider continental and global networks. They deal both with third parties, often in the form of global mandates, and in increasingly integrated intra-corporate networks. Firms such as Black and Decker, Texas Instruments, and Xerox have developed strategies to bolster their market share and profitability in Mexico, while looking beyond the Mexican market. This new environment provides both opportunities and threats. Threats, because benefits earned in protected national economies in exchange for production or other commitments often no longer apply; opportunities, because of the potential of new markets both within the firm and outside it. The bottom line is now competitiveness: "In this new environment," said the president of DEC's Canadian operations, "there are no entitlements. We'll keep our plant and our autonomy if we continue to be competitive."[162] As Mexican and Canadian managers of U.S. firms realize, perhaps this means, first of all, becoming more competitive within the parent firm as the foundation for securing development, production, marketing, and other mandates.

Chapter Six

Mexico and Canada Looking Forward

C anada and Mexico are at vastly different stages in the process of economic development. International agencies rate Canada as the best country in the world to live in, while Mexico struggles to climb out of poverty. Both countries face an array of profound challenges in the last years of the twentieth century. These include difficult political tasks — ensuring that Canada will remain united and that Mexico will become a democratic nation; meeting the social and economic demands of their citizens, particularly for jobs, rising standards of living, and improved quality of life; and maintaining their commitment to succeed in a world of global economic integration and rapid technological change.

In both cases, their economies have become far more deeply integrated into a North American system than anyone might have anticipated only a decade ago. In both cases — although to a much greater extent in Mexico — integration has also been associated with pain and fear. The recession and corporate downsizings in Canada in the early 1990s and the peso crisis and its aftermath in Mexico, together with the impact of increasing global competition, have forced foreign and local companies to reduce excess capacity and surrender the security of protected national markets. The Mexican and Canadian branch economies are all but gone, replaced by a deepening web of intra-company networks, which have intensified the erosion of national boundaries.

Most economists agree that economic integration has produced more macro-economic benefits than costs for Canada and Mexico. Exports, mainly to the United States, have increased remarkably and have been the primary sources of growth in the Canadian and Mexican economies over the past few years. But in both countries, a profound restructuring of the economy is underway that has created losers as well as winners and, in the short term at least, has accentuated inequalities among those groups with and without access to resources more highly valued in the emerging North American economy.

The Mexican Peso Devaluation and Its Aftermath

For Mexico, continental economic integration has been just one element of historic change. Mexico's effort to build a democratic system of government and a modern, export-oriented economy simultaneously has few precedents. Now, as Mexico looks to the future, it must consolidate the economic progress of its recent past and address an array of fundamental, long-standing, and interconnected social, political, and economic problems.

Although some progress toward greater political democracy and income equity was made during the Salinas administration, with more being accomplished on both fronts under the current Zedillo administration, these goals are still largely unrealized. Indeed, these objectives are often cruelly contradictory. Benefits from trade and economic liberalization are spread unevenly among groups and regions. States in the North will gain more, and those in the South are likely to lose more, which will heighten social and political tensions and regional fragmentation. Similarly, while sales of durable goods, like automobiles, to the middle classes have resumed since the 1994 crisis, sales of non-durable goods to poorer groups, such as food, have remained depressed.

Ernesto Zedillo, who became president on December 1, 1994, has faced the task not only of continuing the reforms initiated by the previous two administrations but also of managing the transformation of Mexico from what has been essentially a one-party state to a working democracy. Zedillo's presidency did not begin auspiciously, to say the least. On December 20, 1994, his administration devalued the peso by 45 percent.[163] Concerns that Mexico did not have sufficient liquidity to cover tesobonos (short-term U.S. dollar-denominated government obligations) dominated the early stages of the peso crisis, and the need for widespread structural adjustments was soon apparent. The United States in cooperation with other industrial nations and multilateral lending agencies contributed to a $50 billion aid package to Mexico, which helped retire nearly $30 billion in tesobono debt from the market.[164] The Mexican government was also forced to impose higher taxes and cut spending.

President Zedillo's program of budget cuts, price and tax adjustments, tight monetary policy, and further deregulation and privatization is achieving positive results and setting the stage for what is hoped will be a sustained recovery. Financial market confidence in Mexico, which plummeted so precipitously in early 1995, returned more rapidly than most observers expected. As Finance Minister Guillermo Ortiz observed in October 1997, "It's clear that the recovery has proceeded at a faster pace than had been expected. It's even better than the more optimistic expectations that some analysts had at the beginning of the year."[165] By the summer of 1997, the Bolsa (stock) index had rebounded by more than 60 percent from its February 1995 low, the peso had stabilized, and recent bond offerings had been oversubscribed.

The sinking peso boosted exports, but it is expected that export growth will not be sustained solely through exchange rate mechanisms. The current challenge for Mexico is to create export competitiveness that is not based on the exchange rate or low labor costs, but on efficiency gains and reinvestment.

If Mexico wants high savings, it has to strengthen its currency in order to attract long-term capital to invest in the private sector. Prevailing opinion among economists is that strengthening a currency by overreliance on short-term, speculative capital inflows that increase consumption and decrease the savings rate creates a false sense of economic well-being and leads, inevitably, to financial crisis. Mexico must strengthen its currency instead by instituting tight monetary and fiscal policies, transparency, and improving Central Bank operations, and reforming the banking system. These policies will attract long-term capital (both foreign and local) to the private sector. President Zedillo's economic strategy for the future places primary importance on continued promotion of private investment. But while privatizations are to continue, there are fewer businesses left to sell, and as of mid-1997 there has been some back pedalling by the government — in response to pressure from old-guard Institutional Revolutionary Party (Partido Revolucionario Institucional — PRI) interests. The government ultimately intends to shed all of its holdings except for activities constitutionally reserved for the state. This means that there is little chance that businesses with highly politicized constituencies, such as PEMEX, the state oil company, will be privatized, although there are likely to be more opportunities for the private sector to enter operations such as petrochemicals.

The Impact on NAFTA and U.S. Corporate Operations

The aftermath of the peso crisis deeply affected NAFTA and U.S. corporate operations in Mexico. The massive devaluation of the peso together with preferential tariffs granted by the United States triggered a surge in Mexican exports. While anti-NAFTA groups in the United States capitalized on this as "proof" that the agreement would cause a flood of cheap Mexican imports and result in lost jobs and depressed wages among U.S. workers, both proponents and opponents of NAFTA in Mexico viewed this development positively, as it tended to ease the impact of the devaluation on workers.

Mexico did not revert to old nationalistic policies in the peso crisis. As Sidney Weintraub observed, "NAFTA made it necessary for Mexico to deal with its problems by means other than import restrictions, and this is one reason for the rapid recovery."[166] This revealed how NAFTA had become a cornerstone of Mexican economic policy and has played a vitally important role in locking in critical economic policy changes of the Mexican government.[167]

The silver lining of the peso crisis cloud was that in 1995 Mexico had a more developed economy and was more deeply integrated into the world economy than it was when it faced the debt crisis of 1982.[168] Mexican exports increased, but trade within companies grew more rapidly still. More than 40 percent of Mexican manufactured exports are now sent to parent firms in the United States. To become more competitive, Mexico's firms are exporting goods that are increasingly advanced and capital-intensive rather than labor-intensive. In 1982, oil accounted for 74 percent of Mexico's exports; today, it makes up only 10 percent, while manufactured goods constitute fully 80 percent of total exports. More than 71 percent of Mexico's imports are intermediate goods, 17 percent capital goods, and 12 percent consumer products. This large percentage of intermediate goods reflects the integration of production and marketing that exists between Mexico and the United States.[169] Multinational firms are responsible for most of Mexico's technological exports.

The peso crisis accelerated key structural trends already underway. It put a significant crimp in foreign investment but did not cut it off. Indeed, Mexico has become more attractive to some investors, and the crisis has strengthened rather than diminished the movement toward deeper continental integration. To enhance their competitiveness in the world economy, companies in Mexico are becoming more streamlined, and many are acquiring foreign partners. Foreign firms have spent more than US$7 billion in the past two years, "buying up stakes in everything from a maker of tequila bottles to Mexico's most famous brewer. Mexican companies are increasingly exposed to global competitors and now may have little choice but to become a multinational or marry one."[170] In a quest to become larger, smarter, and international, Mexican companies have determined that the benefits of merging or being acquired exceed the costs of trying to keep afloat in an increasingly competitive global marketplace.Some Mexican businesses are carving out new niches in such areas as high-tech manufacturing. Encouraged by NAFTA, American investors and others are shifting work to Mexico, often to mid-size cities — such as Hermosillo, San Luis Potosí, Querétaro, Saltillo, Aguas Calientes, and Mérida — that will become new growth areas. When the economy was protected, it made sense for companies to serve big consumer markets in Mexico City, Guadalajara, and Monterrey. As Mexico opens up more, companies are opting for points of easy access to supplies and export routes.

While small and mid-size companies were hit hard by an 8 to10 percent plunge in domestic demand, NAFTA provided a cushion for many larger companies and multinational subsidiaries. Despite economic decline and uncertainty, U.S.-Mexican business partnerships have shown steady growth, including production agreements. A closer look at Mexico's trade figures confirms this. Lower demand has reduced imports of consumer goods into Mexico by more than 30 percent since December 1994.[171] But imports of intermediate goods, despite their higher price, have actually increased by almost 7 percent, attributable in large part to their role in the continuing expansion of Mexico's production-sharing sector, which already accounts for half of Mexico's exports to the United States.[172] A growing number of U.S. companies are choosing co-production partnerships with Mexican firms over partners in Asia — despite the peso crisis.

Mexican imports declined sharply after December 1994, but a large base market remains — a population of 90 million consumers, 60 percent of whom are younger than 25. Mexico remains a good market, but not for all products, and U.S. exporters pursue a targeted strategy. Products and services supporting business infrastructure are still doing particularly well. According to R. Sean Randolph, Director of Trade for the State of California, "To modernize and compete in what remains a highly open economy, and to generate dollar income, Mexican businesses must continue buying computers and production machinery."[173] The automotive and consumer goods sectors provide vivid examples of how the interactions among the effects of the peso crisis, NAFTA, and U.S. corporate responses — both strategic and operational — have shaped the new North American business panorama.

The Case of the Automotive Sector

The case of Chrysler shows how firms seek to capture efficiency gains from corporate rationalization, even after the peso crisis. A Chrysler senior executive explained that one of the firm's Mexican plants previously produced several models in relatively small numbers, largely for sale in what was then a protected market that was highly resistant to imports from the United States. He said that within a few years Chrysler plans for this plant to specialize its production on just one model. Larger runs will enable the firms to capture economies of scale that reduce the cost per vehicle. These cars will be sold in Mexico and also exported to the United States. To make a wider range of models available to Mexican consumers, Chrysler will now be able to import autos from the United States. "Our ability to integrate our marketing and our production represents a total operation well beyond what the two could have been separately," he concluded.[174]

The peso crisis has shifted Mexico's role in the North American economy from a vast new market to a vast new production site. "Mexico has not become the thriving consumer market envisioned by NAFTA's promoters. Instead, driven by a seemingly unlimited supply of cheap labor, Mexico has emerged as an export base for cars, trucks, and parts more swiftly and dramatically than anyone imagined."[175] Before NAFTA, the Mexican auto industry projected domestic sales of cars and trucks at 1.2 million vehicles by 2002 and estimated that exports would account for only one third of the domestic output of vehicles. In 1995, domestic sales were only 185,000 vehicles, however, while exports had increased to 781,000. In 1996, sales in Mexico rose to 334,000 units, while exports soared to 975,000.

The peso crisis forced other companies to restructure their Mexican strategies in a similar fashion. For example, a Goodyear factory that had imported supplies but exported not a single tire in 1992 exported half of its production by 1995, mostly to the United States, with some going to South America and Europe as well. "From one day to another we passed from being an importer company to an exporter company," said the plant's production chief.[176] This Goodyear branch plant faced a possible threat from NAFTA — because Goodyear would lose the Mexican tariff that had protected it from more efficient U.S. competition. In response, Goodyear cut its workforce from 2,500 to 2,000 and raised its output from 12,500 tires per day in 1992 to 14,500 per day in 1994. Local sales increased, but the firm was forced to identify new markets. In 1993, Goodyear had begun to ship 7 percent of its output to the United States — and increased this to 20 percent in 1994 — after the NAFTA tariff cuts. The peso devaluation forced Goodyear to make a much more radical shift in direction: in 1995, it exported half of its production. Suddenly, from being a platform to supply rising Mexican demand, albeit with some exports, exports became its primary thrust. The peso devaluation provided not only the necessity for change but also the means. "The devaluation," said the plant's logistics director, "helped us to become competitive." Before devaluation, the plant received the same output for $0.90 that it received in the United States for $1.00. After devaluation, it received the same output in Mexico for $0.62 cents.[177]

Some companies responded to the peso crisis by shifting production to Mexico to take advantage of the new low-cost structure. Cummins Engine's sales of its heavy-duty truck and bus engines fell in Mexico by 98 percent following the devaluation. Its response was to switch a production line from Brazil to Mexico to create a new export platform that would capture the gains in cost reduction created by the devaluation.[178]

Ford was the first Big Three automaker to reorganize to support a continental strategy in the late 1980s. Ford restructured one of its Mexican plants to produce the Mystique and Contour cars, together with some light trucks, for both the domestic and export markets. Imports from Ford's U.S. plants would meet the demand in Mexico for other models. Ford's post-devaluation correction was to do whatever was possible to sell some cars in Mexico while boosting exports and cutting costs to contain losses. Ford's domestic sales in Mexico fell by 50 percent in 1995, but exports increased by 22 percent. The company stripped out extras to reduce the price of domestic models while shifting some auto parts business to Mexico. Just a year after the peso crisis, in November 1995, Ford said it was planning to go forward with $450 million in new investments to retool plants and boost component production.[179]

To implement this strategy effectively, automakers (and others as well) must reduce the percentage of inputs that are imported. The automotive industry in Mexico faces a major problem: because such a high percentage of inputs are imported, the price of the finished product does not fully reflect the impact of peso devaluation. The potential gains of devaluation could be realized if a greater proportion of parts were made in Mexico, assuming a sufficient scale to produce necessary economies as well, of course, as required levels of quality. Mexico also would have to export more parts if these levels of scale were to be achieved.

The Consumer Goods Sector

While the days of Mexican consumers freely snapping up imported goods are gone and are unlikely to return soon, this does not mean that Mexican consumers have stopped buying altogether. The devaluation and its fallout forced some U.S retailers who were just beginning to set up shop in Mexico, such as J.C. Penney, Dillards, K-Mart, and Wal-Mart, to reevaluate their expansion plans.[180] Reevaluation, however, is not synonymous with cancellation. Despite the turmoil, few U.S. businesses have abandoned the Mexican market. After increasing investment in Mexico by 50 percent, to $31 billion since 1991, U.S. retailers are reluctant to walk away from the costly distribution systems and brand awareness they have built up. For now, marketers are repositioning their brands for an economy still in the grip of austerity. They are raising the proportion of domestically produced goods as the price of imports soars, adjusting ad strategies, and working to help local distributors stay afloat. With the peso stabilizing and purchasing power recovering, some companies have viewed the crisis as a chance to seize market share. Market leader Coca-Cola, under fierce attack from PepsiCo, has gone ahead with plans to roll out Fresca, while Nestlé is continuing a planned assault on the supermarket ice cream segment. In August 1997, J.C. Penney announced that it would resume its expansion and complete outlets in Mexico City and Guadalajara by 1999.[181] According to Peter Economides, CEO of McCann-Erickson's Mexican subsidiary, the country's largest ad agency, "Long term, this is still a very good place to do business."[182]

No longer flocking to expensive imports, Mexicans are turning to familiar names, core brands, and value for their money. Wal-Mart, for example, with 11 superstores and 22 Sam's Wholesale Clubs in Mexico, advertises Mexican products proudly.[183] Even companies that manufacture in Mexico, such as Nabisco and Kraft Food, Inc., are seeing costs rise. The hardest task has been to maintain distribution. Imported capital goods and components for production are now costlier, as is the transfer price of services purchased from the parent company, other subsidiaries, and vendors. The pool of local suppliers to these multinational firms has shrunk, further increasing the cost of sourcing and squeezing operating profit margins.

Since the peso devaluation, Mexican retailers prefer to run out of stock rather than carry inventory. Many companies, therefore, are adopting a strategy of "frequent delivery." Firms are also experimenting with different product mixes and pricing policies to adjust to a poorer consumer market. For instance, as consumers began switching to generic brands, Procter & Gamble responded with "reduced price" packages that contain fewer items than the previous presentations. Other sectors are following. Milk processors have introduced a 0.75 liter presentation at the same price as their former 1 liter cartons.[184] In addition, to reduce their exchange-rate risk, companies are trying to pass the risk onto suppliers and customers. Computer distributors, for example, now quote prices in dollars. The ability to offer accessible credit plans to woo back customers is also a key to successful competition in Mexico.[185]

Producers able to shift to export sales have partially compensated for lower local demand. Many U.S. multinational companies in Mexico have compensated for the collapse of domestic demand by sending goods abroad. The explanation for this is the depreciated peso: these companies saw their labor costs in dollars fall by more than one third in 1995-1996. The resulting flood into the United States of cheaper autos, televisions, and other products, including tires, turned a 1994 $1.4 billion U.S. trade surplus with Mexico into a $15 billion deficit.[186] A growing boon to consumer goods producers will be the 30 million U.S. citizens of Hispanic descent. Companies such as Colgate-Palmolive are leveraging their Mexican brands in the United States. This firm is marketing its Suavital brand fabric softener and Fabuloso hard surface cleaner to U.S. Hispanics in a national campaign.[187] Other companies, like Kimberly Clark de Mexico (43 percent U.S-owned) have gained market share owing to import substitution and the collapse of marginal competitors. This is attributed to Kimberly's market dominance, leverage with retailers, and broad product portfolio that includes both premium and low-cost "value" brands. The firm also cut costs aggressively throughout the recession.[188]

In late summer of 1997, Procter and Gamble (P&G) acquired Lorreto y Peña Pobre (LyPP) for $170 million, providing P&G with a solid point of entry into the Mexican tissue market, and Kimberly Clark de México merged with Compañía Industrial San Cristóbal, a unit of Scott Paper, thereby nailing down leadership in most areas of the paper products market in Mexico.[189]

The Road Ahead

The peso crisis and its aftermath have forced many businesses operating in Mexico to restructure and shift their short-term strategies — by adjusting their pricing and supply policy, hedging exchange risk exposure, cutting costs, and offering financing.[190] It created new incentives and new limitations as well. The crisis intensified fears among some groups that NAFTA would be destabilizing and punitive for many Mexicans. One highly critical report argues that NAFTA's impact on agriculture has been worse than envisioned, with exports increasing by 63 percent between 1993 and 1996 and imports surging ahead by 87.4 percent in the same period. Additionally, the report says, better and more plentiful jobs have not materialized, job growth has been sluggish and unstable, and many workers continue to find it difficult to form unions.[191]

It is too soon to make any final evaluation of the above charges. The impact of NAFTA and the peso crisis will not be clear for years. Most analysts feel that while there clearly have been negative results, the positive impact will prove more profound, changing indelibly the political economies of both Mexico and North America. These include broader and sharper implementation of liberal fiscal and monetary policies, improved and transparent regulatory frameworks, increased privatization, more efficient public administration, and the adoption of local and multinational corporate strategic and operational policies aimed at successfully responding to the continual challenge of continental and global economic integration.

Multinational firms, along with their partners (both foreign and local), suppliers, and distributors, are well positioned — regardless of macroeconomic slips and slides along the way — to capitalize upon the advantages of North American economic integration, Mexico's large consumer market, cost and production capabilities to serve export markets, and a factor endowment mix (including technology) that enhances their position as units within upstream and downstream corporate networks.

The most serious threats to this scenario are created by social and political conditions in Mexico. Here, too, NAFTA and the peso crisis affected (and were affected by) long-standing problems in these areas. Severe social inequality and seven and one-half decades of one-party rule are inarguable impediments to Mexico's capacity to maximize its economic and commercial potential, objectives that can only be realized fully through democracy, social equity, and democratic capitalism. While the Zedillo administration recovery program seems to be moving in the right direction, the government's economic policies must focus more on the alleviation of poverty. According to INEGI, the Mexican government's statistical agency, the wealthiest 10 percent of the population controlled 41 percent of the nation's wealth in 1996. The government's social service agency estimated last year that 42 million people, or 46 percent of the population, lived in poverty and another 22 million lived in extreme poverty.[192] As the Chiapas uprising in 1994 revealed, Mexico's political system is still vulnerable to shocks if reforms continue to offer little in the way of improvement in the standard of living for the country's lower classes. For many, the route to greater economic equity lies in political reform.

Mexico is moving in the right direction. The movement toward greater democracy was underlined in September 1997, when Mexico's first opposition-dominated Congress in seven decades opened. Opposition parties won a 261-seat majority in the 500-member Chamber of Deputies in the July 6, 1997, election. Professor Rafael Fernández de Castro observed that the recent mid-term elections "represent a watershed in the process of democratizing Mexico. . . . Analysts agree that the political reforms of 1977 set in motion a transition to democracy. But the advances of the last 20 years appear small when compared with the results of the July 6th election."[193] The opposition parties, the left-of-center Democratic Revolutionary Party (Partido de la Revolución Democrática — PRD), and the pro-business

National Action Party (Partido Acción Nacional — PAN), although ideological opposites, are united in their belief that economic stability, policies to encourage savings and investments, and modernization and opening to the economy are essential for Mexico. As Mexico looks forward, there is every hope that political and social reform, coupled with the economic and commercial liberalization underway, will contribute to the further expansion, broadening, and enrichment of the environment in which corporations operate.

Despite uncertainties about the impact of Mexico's policy of liberalization and economic integration, the government has moved aggressively to extend free trade linkages in the Western Hemisphere. Mexico now has free trade agreements with Chile (signed before NAFTA) and Costa Rica; it also has an agreement with the Group of Three (Bolivia, Colombia, and Venezuela). Mexico is negotiating a free trade agreement with Guatemala, Honduras, and El Salvador, while bilateral negotiations are underway with Nicaragua, Panama, Ecuador, and Peru and with Chile for expanding their bilateral agreement. Negotiations are continuing as well with MERCOSUR for a transitional arrangement to replace the existing agreement under the Latin American Integration Association, which will then serve as a basis for broader negotiations, perhaps to be wrapped into the creation of a Free Trade Area of the Americas by 2005.

Canada and a North American Economic Space

In the first years following Canada's free trade agreement with the United States (CUSFTA), in the midst of a deep recession, some Canadians wondered if their worst fears of the 1970s — dependency, truncation, and the loss of autonomy — had indeed materialized. In 1991, Maude Barlow and Bruce Campbell, well-known economic nationalists, published a familiar rhetoric of economic dependence and class conflict. "Canada," they wrote, "is the most economically occupied country in the industrial world; no other country even comes close. More than half our manufacturing sector is under foreign control. We have learned from years of experience that, left to their own devices, foreign corporations may act contrary to Canadian economic interests, destroying more jobs than they create, and killing off Canadian competitors. They import more, export less, and are less likely to use local suppliers than are Canadian firms."[194]

Free trade, Barlow and Campbell claimed, was leading to the "warehousing" of Canada. "The withdrawal of obligation of foreign companies to produce in Canada has dramatically changed U.S. subsidiaries here. Rather than becoming export platforms into the new continental market, branch manufacturing plants are simply shutting down. If they leave anything behind, it is just a warehouse or a sales office. The Canadian market can now be supplied merely by adding an extra shift or by filling unused capacity at a U.S. or Mexican plant."[195] Interestingly enough, the instigators of this plot are not the U.S. multinationals. Instead, Barlow and Campbell pointed to "the Conservative/corporate action plan to dismantle the country" as the real source of this misguided effort. They contended that the economic crisis of the early 1990s was no accident; it was "the planned consequence of policies executed since 1984 by the Conservative government in alliance with big business, in order to change radically the Canadian economy. Brian Mulroney; his Tory cabinet; and the Business Council for National Issues (BCNI), the cabinet of big corporations led by Thomas d'Aquino, set out to transform the Canadian economy from a distinctly national to a regional one within an integrated continental economy dominated by the United States."[196]

In fact, by this time, the familiar indictment was no longer drawing much blood. In the 1993 general election, the Liberal Party, led by Jean Chrétien, gained a surprising majority in the House of Commons. The Liberals had desperately opposed the free trade agreement with the United States in the 1988 election, but in Parliament, they had made no efforts to undermine it. In the 1993 general election, neither the Liberals nor any other party opposed CUSFTA or the new North American Free Trade Agreement. Economic nationalist groups were largely shut out of the 1993 election, and while the New Democratic Party regained a few seats in 1997, economic nationalism played no significant role in the general elections of 1993 or 1997. As J. L. Granatstein observed, "The Chrétien Liberals read the public mood correctly — there would be no more desperate campaigns attacking American influence in mainstream Canadian politics. Chrétien refused to make NAFTA a major issue in the general election of 1993, instead promising only 'side deals' to improve deficient parts of the trade agreement. When the Liberals formed a majority government after the vote, no significant changes in government trade policy were expected, and predictably none were offered...."[197]

Chrétien's government not only ratified NAFTA but has taken a very vigorous lead in efforts to expand it. The Liberal government has pushed to include Chile in NAFTA — and has struck its own free trade deal with Chile — and has begun the process of building a Free Trade Area of the Americas by 2005. In April 1997, the government announced that it would seek to negotiate free trade pacts throughout Latin America, without waiting for the United States to take the lead in hemispheric trade liberalization. Said then trade minister Art Eggleton, "'We're going to certainly move ahead with our relationships in Latin America. If we wait, we will be left behind."[198]

What happened to change Canadian minds so dramatically on free trade? Resignation, information, and success seem to be the key elements that have driven change in attitudes. Canadians increasingly agree that exports are critical for continued economic growth and that trade protectionism cannot be maintained in this new environment. The great majority of Canadians believe that the United States will continue to be Canada's largest market, and many feel it will become even more important than it is now. Some 46 percent of Canadians in a recent poll evaluated NAFTA's impact as very or somewhat positive. Less than one third — only 31 percent — rated NAFTA as very or somewhat negative.[199] "People have absorbed free trade," observed Senator Allan MacEachen, a nationalist Liberal. "It, and the global economy, are now taken for granted."[200] These attitudes are also a response to Canada's success in North American trade over the past decade. Canadian exports to the United States have more than doubled from $105 billion in 1988 to an expected $245 billion in 1997. Gordon Ritchie, one of the key Canadian negotiators of CUSFTA, wrote, "Canada's trade and investment performance over the past few years has been nothing short of spectacular, and the forecasts are for more of the same well into the third millennium." The reasons for such success, he says, boil down to this, "The Canadian economy has regained a high degree of cost competitiveness, which has put it in a position to reap the rewards of free trade with the U.S."[201]

Free trade has been widely accepted among Canadians, and political opposition to deeper economic integration has declined. The influence of traditional anti-Americanism and Barlow-Campbell-style economic nationalism in Canadian politics is also much more limited. However, many Canadians still remain fearful about the impact that free trade and rising levels of economic integration with the United States will have on their country and culture.

According to Rebecca Goldfarb's research, this reluctance can be seen in several key sectors of Canada's economy still characterized by powerful resistance to liberalization and economic integration — in telecommunications, some parts of financial services, media-broadcasting, and Canada's "cultural" industries, for example. In these sectors, viewed by many as supporting the remaining core of Canadian identity, liberalization has moved forward slowly and inconsistently. Policy with regard to broadcasting, "Canada's premier cultural policy," and in these other sectors as well illustrate "Canadian preservation objectives and the external constraints on these public policy goals."[202]

The concerns of many informed Canadians about North American economic integration today have less to do with theory than with practice. The need to overcome inefficiencies and to eliminate duplicated and excess capacity is widely accepted. Few believe that an import-substitution economy can compete successfully in the global economy of the twenty-first century. Concerns emerge, however, from uncertainty about the role, sensitivity, and reliability of the United States in this new environment.

Risk for Canadian business is inherent in North American integration. Trade disputes and a wide array of border irritations continue to roil the bilateral relationship and annoy — or outrage — Canadians. Another risk is that the Canadian operations of U.S. firms, even if they remain open, would be collapsed into existing U.S. structures instead of becoming part of a true North American entity, meaning that Canadian units might report directly to U.S. — not North American — business units. Responsiveness to conditions in Canada could deteriorate, with Canadian operations left to pick up the crumbs. Canadian managers and employees alike would be justifiably frustrated and angry.

This has certainly occurred in some firms, and in these cases, the Canadian role in new North American business systems has been downgraded. This has been more likely when U.S. firms have adopted more decentralized structures, in which most operating authority has been transferred to U.S.-based business units that have then centralized their operations. In this sort of "silo" structure, decisions are driven by the particular needs of the individual business units, and no one in the parent organization has responsibility for thinking about Canada as a whole. It is useful to recall that this sort of rationalization and restructuring is not a phenomenon that affects Canadian subsidiaries alone, however. Sometimes overlooked is the fact that the restructuring of Canadian industry is a dimension (relatively limited from the perspective of many U.S. headquarters) of a pattern of corporate reorganization on a continental and even global basis. What is often viewed from Canada as an isolated and U.S-engineered restructuring of the Canadian economy is in reality a part of a much wider process.[203]

This new environment also gives rise to fears of a kind of southward corporate brain-drain — that "many of Canada's best and brightest managers are leaving the country in search of better opportunities elsewhere."[204] Often, these opportunities are found within the same firm but in the United States. However, the movement is not all in one direction. U.S. managers are also streaming north to take senior positions in Canadian companies. "At current rates of importation," writes Canadian journalist Rod McQueen, "Canadian boardrooms will soon resemble Canada's professional baseball and football squads — peopled in the main with players from the U.S."[205] But there is no evidence to suggest that any of these developments are inevitable or that they are the ultimate intentions of U.S. parent firms.

The Changing Shape of NAFTA

In Mexico, the impact of the peso crisis has been to strengthen rather than retard the movement toward deeper continental integration, just as the impact of recession in the early 1990s was to strengthen Canadian resolve to compete more effectively in an increasingly competitive continental and international economy. Yet, the configuration of the North American economic system is likely to be different than was anticipated just a few years ago.

When NAFTA was first discussed, proponents assumed that rapidly expanding markets in Mexico and rising levels of demand for a wide range of products guaranteed that continental integration would be a win-win game. Production in Mexico would increase substantially, and Mexican exports would grow rapidly, particularly to the United States and increasingly to Canada. At the same time, it was predicted that increases in consumption and rising purchasing power in Mexico would ensure that production and employment in the United States and Canada would not suffer. Mexico would export more, but it would also import much more. Jobs would be shifted around. Some East Asian jobs might be lost as production migrated to Mexico. Proponents believed that few jobs would be lost in North America. For North American workers, the prospects were that increased efficiency due to integration would lead to higher wages and then to more jobs.

The impact of NAFTA is different from what was anticipated in 1993. The overall results are likely to be the same or similar to those predicted, but in a substantially longer time frame. The earlier model of NAFTA assumed that continental integration would be a relatively painless process. The key would be to increase production and consumption in Mexico at the same time, using foreign capital rather than Mexican savings. This was the magic of a win-win solution. The newer answer is more taxing. Mexicans have had to reduce their consumption, while producing and exporting more. And they have had to rely much more on their own savings to make this happen. If Mexico imports less and exports more, employment will increase more slowly in the United States and Canada, and some blue-collar production jobs will be transferred to Mexico.

But the new model is scarcely zero sum. Mexico's middle class is growing, and U.S. and Canadian exports to Mexico have increased substantially. U.S. exports to Mexico increased by 36.5 percent from 1993 to 1996, and by 1996, one-third of the United States' total two-way trade in goods was with Canada and Mexico.[206] There is no painless solution, but a more prosperous Mexico offers its North American partners enormous opportunities for economic growth.

NAFTA involved commitments on environmental, social, and labor policies as well as trade and investment. The failure to achieve significant gains in these areas has drawn much criticism from labor and environmentalist groups. Others argue that the NAFTA supplemental agreements, the North American Agreement for Environmental Cooperation (NAAEC) and the North American Accord for Labor Cooperation (NAALC), along with the establishment of the Commission for Environmental Cooperation (CEC), the Commission for Labor Cooperation (CLC), and the North American Accord for Labor Cooperation (NAALC), have contributed to incremental progress in both the environmental and labor areas. The fact is, however, as trade economist Sidney Weintraub points out, "The time has been much too brief and the circumstances too unfavorable for substantial accomplishment," particularly in light of the peso crisis. There is little reliable evidence to date that labor and environmental conditions in Mexico since NAFTA have deteriorated, improved significantly, or remained the same.[207]

While substantial numbers of Mexicans and Canadians harbor deep concerns about the likely impact of NAFTA, most leaders and key organizations in both countries have come to accept the reality of continental economic integration. This may not be true, however, in the United States. Mexicans and Canadians are alarmed by the tide of inwardness and defensive economic nationalism that has become increasingly widespread in their predominant NAFTA partner. Opposition to NAFTA and its extension to Chile and the rest of the Western Hemisphere in the United States has centered on fears of lost jobs and concerns that U.S. firms would pull up stakes and head south. In the case of Mexico, concerns focus on immigration and ethnicity as well. Fears that trade agreements like NAFTA will erode U.S. sovereignty are also widespread. One of Canada's leading journalists, Andrew Cohen, recently having arrived in Washington, asked, "Is the United States turning inward? Is it still to shoulder responsibilities as the world's only superpower?" Developments in Washington, he observed, "... have raised fears of a creeping neo-isolationism — or at least a parochialism — in American foreign policy at the very time its military, economic and political power are wholly unchallenged." In the same article, Cohen cites recent polls showing that 69 percent of U.S. citizens feel that imports should be restricted to protect jobs, 67 percent believe that jobs created by trade are low paying, and 61 percent are against fast-track authority.[208]

A leading Mexican student of U.S. politics, testifying before a U.S. Congressional Subcommittee on the Western Hemisphere, could give the United States at best a "B-" for fulfilling its obligations agreed to under the NAFTA accords. "The list of evasions of NAFTA commitments," he recounted, "includes tomatoes, circulation of Mexican trucks in the states that adjourn Mexico, avocados, pork, and cement among others."[209] A U.S.-Canada free trade arrangement was discussed any number of times in the postwar era, but, as William Diebold observed, "For various well-known reasons the idea of overall free trade with the United States seems not to have been regarded as politically acceptable in Canada."[210] For Mexicans, free trade with the United States could scarcely be considered until the early 1980s. Only the impact of dramatic changes in the global environment led Canada and Mexico to accept the need for free trade in North America during the late 1980s and 1990s. Now, however, as efforts are underway to deepen arrangements that have been made in CUSFTA and NAFTA and to extend free trade agreements into Latin America, it is Canada and Mexico that are more enthusiastic and the United States that is holding back.

Chapter Seven

Corporate Organization in a New North American Economy

Patterns of corporate organization in North America are undergoing extensive change. Until a few years ago, national requirements, national systems, and national responsiveness were the key factors in determining subsidiary structures and strategies. Today, every dimension of corporate organization is influenced by a wider array of forces, and many more strategic and organizational options are available to firms than ever before.

Patterns of Local Sensitivity

The root-and-branch economic nationalist paradigm provided little space to analyze specific patterns of corporate organization and strategy. However, there are other serious "national," if not nationalist, perspectives with regard to the relationship between headquarters and subsidiaries that are relevant to current North American trends and patterns in corporate organization.

A 1993 article by Canadian academics Julian Birkinshaw and Warren Ritchie, for example, examines multinational corporate organizational issues from a subsidiary perspective. The authors seek to assess the balance of costs and benefits that result from efforts to capture efficiency gains through intra-corporate integration. They argue that while no one denies that the branch plant system led to inefficiencies and duplication, there is still a very strong need for national responsiveness, and they contend that the "... consolidated North American form taken by many multinationals in the past few years represents, for some, an overcorrection to the pressures for integration." For both the subsidiary and the corporation as a whole, according to Birkinshaw and Ritchie, there are dangers in taking this model too far: "For the subsidiary, cross-border consolidation challenges its right to exist, at least as something more substantial than a regional sales office. For the corporation, there are concerns that local-market sensitivity and important investment opportunities are being overlooked."[211]

Birkinshaw and Ritchie believe that national differences, both in terms of employee and customer characteristics, are not disappearing. National differences can be embodied in unique core competencies, those attributes and skills that allow a firm to outperform its competitors continually, and it is the country unit that has the potential to become the natural home for these core competencies. Country operations can thus become key elements of competitive advantage in the contest among multinational corporations (MNCs), even when economies of scale are modest.[212]

These are wise words of caution, especially with regard to the continuing need for local sensitivity. But the implicit model on which these comments rest is an increasingly obsolescent, state-centered paradigm.[213] The new architecture of North America, in our view, creates a much more complex problem of defining markets and maintaining sensitivities than this state-centered paradigm suggests.

Responsiveness, of course, is essential to business success. "Think global, act local" is the most commonplace of business admonitions. It is not clear, however, that the need for national responsiveness is greater than the need for regional responsiveness. Specifically, the fundamental question is whether there remains or in the future will be a distinctly U.S., Mexican, or Canadian national market in each business sector. Operational boundaries for some firms will still, of course, be defined by national regulations such as health, safety, and environmental standards. In the chemical industry, for example, one major U.S. company states that 75 percent of its income in Canada in the 1990s will continue to come from products regulated by the Canadian government.[214] Similarly, the boundaries of other markets may be powerfully influenced by national historical experience, culture, and language. This will be the case in various Mexican markets for the foreseeable future. Some aspects of taste and style are shaped by national preferences. Taste and style, however, may be defined increasingly in terms of subnational regions or even local area. Some of these regions may even cross national borders. A "Cascadian" lifestyle, for example, seems to characterize North America's Pacific Northwest — which includes Oregon, Washington, and British Columbia. Patterns of business are similar in the region, combining natural resources, high technology, and tourism; and people there share distinctive shared styles and interests. Similarly, an economic region with substantial shared styles and tastes seems to be emerging along the U.S.-Mexican border.[215]

Forecasts like this are obviously fragile, which is why successful marketing consultants are well paid. The baseline point, however, is that within North America there are elements of global markets, continental markets, markets defined by traditional national borders, and markets defined by regional tastes and interests, some of which cross national borders. Firms are gearing up to work on this more complex, multi-layered gameboard. Given these emerging patterns, it does not seem reasonable to assume that a U.S. firm's Canadian headquarters located in Toronto or its Mexican office in Mexico City or Monterrey, for example, would provide the necessary responsiveness to the full array of these complex and changing environments. This is hardly a new idea. Those who are responsible for marketing are well aware of regional differences throughout North America — and utterly aware that a corporate map of North American markets would not be made up of three distinct and homogeneous national economies.[193] The need for corporations to maintain high levels of sensitivity to local needs does not stand as an argument for the recreation of older, national systems of subsidiary organization, although it does require innovative strategic and organizational solutions.[216]

The Corporate Map of North America

The corporate "map" of North America is being redrawn in other ways as well. With regard to production, for example, the situation has changed enormously and has critically altered the operations of subsidiaries within what were recently far more integrated national economies. Sourcing inputs for the production process are now organized by a wide range of variables. Manufacturers can choose to source inputs from a global supermarket, but they must constantly be aware of competitive advantage and disadvantage inherent in each choice. Manufacturers can deal, for example, with the lowest cost supplier in another continent. They can also opt to source from nearby suppliers, where constant interaction can be maintained. Higher prices might be offset in these situations by firmer control over quality and by the opportunity for closer collaboration in product planning and development. What has changed is the much wider array of strategic options for organizing the value chain that now exist in many industries.

The movement toward outsourcing and the emergence of "networked" structured organizations further change the nature of the relationship between corporate parents and overseas subsidiaries and between the firm and host or home countries. Significant functions can be outsourced, and alliances or other kinds of relationships can take the place of direct investments. In the automotive industry, for example, parts and systems manufacturers, such as the Canadian firm Magna, have become increasingly important players as major assemblers have outsourced substantial elements of their production process.

James Brian Quinn writes that manufacturing is no longer the core function, even for product producers: "Thanks to new technologies, executives can divide up their companies' value chains, handle the key strategic elements internally, outsource others advantageously anywhere in the world with minimal transaction costs, and yet coordinate all essential activities more effectively to meet customers' needs."[217] Successful product makers have organized themselves as "intellectual holding companies" that purposively manufacture as little internally as possible. Other models move even further in this direction. The British management guru Charles Handy says that companies of the future will consist of "a web of alliances, joint ventures, arrangements and pacts. More risks will have to be shared. Companies will have centers but rather than head offices, they will be small centers designed on the principle of 'reverse delegation' with the center doing only what the parts on their own cannot do and which they, therefore, delegate to the center. Companies will be federations of bits and pieces, joined together in different ways for different purposes."[218]

This movement toward outsourcing and network or alliance-based production has generated significant counter tides. As one U.S. executive observed of his company, "At one point, a few years back before our total quality and benchmarking programs were put in place, there was a much greater possibility that we would outsource something. But we have become much more efficient. The practice of benchmarking and quality management have made it so we are now the ones who are most competitive. We can manufacture at world class levels instead of someone outside doing it for us."[219] In all of these issues, however, the bottom line is that "national" considerations matter less and less, and it becomes more and more difficult to answer Robert Reich's question "who is us?"

Similarly, relations with governments also have changed. Competition among units within the same firm for mandates and for the right to survive intensifies as firms adopt new technologies and in other ways slim down in a more competitive environment. National as well as state, provincial, and local polities seek to influence the outcome of this competition through a wide array of direct and indirect vehicles — including infrastructure development (transportation, communications, education, and training) and tax deals. Corporate units draw upon whatever national, provincial, state, and local public policy resources they can to assemble their own versions of a "cluster of excellence." In various cases, local factors in a city or metropolitan region may have greater weight in determining how various pieces fit together to create or fail to create a cluster for a particular set of firms. Where public policy charges off in the "wrong" direction (with regard to taxes, for example, or environmental policies) or when governments are dead broke, the task will be tougher — but adversity may also stimulate innovation. "Smarter" governments will work more closely with key firms and other constituencies such as labor to improve the public policy environment and help business units in their area win mandates.

U.S. branch plants in Mexico and Canada have been transformed into subsidiary operations that must survive within the production network of their parent firms. The role of these subsidiaries is being increasingly shaped by intra-firm competition for access to research, development, production and marketing mandates, capital, and the development of new products. Rationalization of these operations is likely to continue, becoming a permanent part of the subsidiary's day-to-day existence. Mexican and Canadian firms have changed as well, reacting in similar ways to the same forces as foreign-owned firms.

At times, the reorganization of firms is explained solely, it appears, in terms of the siting of production. Canadian critics of the CUSFTA as well as U.S. critics of NAFTA have argued that these agreements give foreign-owned firms the perfect incentive to cease manufacturing in Canada or that NAFTA would lead U.S. firms to abandon U.S. locations in search of lower cost factors of production. This scenario rests on the view that the location of production is determined primarily by the cost of factors of production, particularly labor and the regulatory environment, and that Mexico naturally would become an industrialist's dream with cheap labor and a questionable commitment to environmental protection.

While the above scenario has been played out in some cases, it has not reached the proportions opponents of CUSFTA and NAFTA predicted. Because the entire production process is undergoing change in response to global competition, it is simply wrong to think that what determines locational decisions are how cheap wages are or how much environmental pillage a company can get away with. If this were the case, U.S. firms would have abandoned Canada long before the CUSFTA ever came into being, and Mexico and Haiti would be among the leading exporters in the entire world.

Firms will continue to develop and manufacture in the United States and Canada, as well as in other countries with high wage costs and strict enforcement of environmental regulations, because these countries possess the infrastructure and the human capital — people with skills, knowledge, experience, and commitment to business success — that more than make up for cost advantages of Mexico and other low-wage countries. If there are losers in the NAFTA project, they may be the industrializing nations of Asia; evidence shows that Mexico is already beginning to siphon business from North American firms that had previously done business with Asian newly industrialized countries (NICs). More to the point, Mexico will succeed in the future by competing successfully for high value-added, high-skilled, and high-paying jobs — not for jobs at the low end of the value-added, skill, and pay range.

In our view, the restructuring occurring today is more complex than in the postwar era, affecting the fundamentals of industrial production and business management. The proper analogy is the industrial revolution in production and corporate systems in the 1880s and 1890s, which led to the rise of mass production and the system of industrial capitalism, changing the entire system. Today we are experiencing another paradigm shift, evidence of which is widespread. The corporate giants of the United States, companies such as GM and IBM that were viewed as the symbols of U.S. post-war industrial capitalism, are deeply engaged in struggles that go well beyond the problem of weak markets. Even as economic recovery has strengthened, many of North America's most important firms continue to search for strategies and organizational structures that will ensure competitiveness (and in some cases survival) in the new global business dynamic. To understand the reactions of firms to the new competitive dynamic, we may be required to set aside most of what we have learned about production and organizational strategies. We are now viewing the emergence of a new system of production that, under current definitions, is not so much "lean" as "agile" or "flexible." New technologies do not so much provide tools to improve the capacities of older systems of production (for example, General Motors' early unsuccessful efforts to automate processes in its plants) as shape whole systems of production. New technologies have a profound impact on the nature of labor in the production process, skills required by that process, relations with suppliers and purchasers, decisions managers make, and management systems that are most effective, given these changes.

As the nature of the production process is transformed, so too are the structures that organize the process. To be sure, changes and innovations in technology have generated vast uncertainties about the emerging shape of new corporate and management systems. Emerging organizational and management systems seem to combine elements of centralization and decentralization. Both higher levels of intra-firm integration and greater autonomy of certain business units within firms seem to coexist in many firms today.

Management expert Handy captures the essence of the problem of reorganizing firms in this new environment, if not the clarity of a solution. The paradox of how to be big but also small dominates business and politics today, he says:

> In business, federalism is not simple decentralization with the center acting as a banker to the separate businesses like the conglomerates of old. That loses the advantages of scale, of being able to develop lead technologies across a range of separate businesses, of combining to purchase or bid for a major contract that

might involve the skills of several businesses. But neither is federalism a simple divisionalization, the grouping of businesses under sets of umbrellas. That leaves too much power in the hands of those holding the umbrellas and pays too little attention to local needs or to the knowledge and contacts of those out in the marketplace. Nor is it a matter of simply empowering those in the front line or in separate countries. That ignores the expertise of people farther back or in other groupings. Federalism responds to all these pressures, balancing power among those in the center of the organization, those in the centers of expertise and those in the center of the action, the operating businesses.[220]

The paradox, as Handy calls it, indicates a crucial point: the emergence of forms of corporate organizational structures, designed to establish a new balance between centralization and autonomy in North America and elsewhere. In the case of North America in particular, just as U.S. firms seem to be clawing Canadian operations back into U.S. (or North American) systems, the weight of the U.S. core seems to be diminishing within the global organization. In the words of one executive, the idea of the moment is "a very lean head office, with a family of more independent and flexible businesses around it."[221] The objective is to establish the best balance and maximize efficiency between centralized strategic control and local autonomy. In these new systems, local managerial autonomy increases on some scales and decreases on others.

Looking Toward the Year 2000: An Integrated Corporate System in North America?

As we look toward the year 2000, are we going to see an integrated corporate system in North America? It seems to us that the answer to this question is almost surely "yes." Intensifying competition on a global scale forces companies to eliminate excess capacity and rationalize production operations in every possible fashion. The rapid pace of technological innovation provides a dramatic array of new vehicles for management and coordination as well as production and distribution. We can forecast with confidence that rationalization and integration will be key parameters of change in corporate structures and strategies in North America in the coming years.

The findings of this study, together with its two predecessors, confirm that even before the ratification of NAFTA, a North American perspective had emerged in many firms' strategic outlooks. It seems clear that many U.S. firms will continue to meet global competition by rationalizing production systems and eliminating excess capacity in North America and by putting in place more integrated continental organizations.

Different Perceptions of a North American System

The shape of the emerging North American system may be more varied and complex than anticipated, however. Many of the firms studied in the three surveys described in this book had created or were in the midst of organizing North American divisions, operations, and business units designed to integrate Canadian and then Mexican branch plants into wider systems. However, no single approach seems to have emerged as a model. Instead, we have seen high levels of organizational innovation and experimentation. Some companies seem to have undergone a number of reorganizations, both within their North American operations and globally.

Indeed, by the mid-1990s, some companies were no longer certain whether their North American operations should be viewed as fundamental elements of strategies or whether they were more likely to be viewed as transient steps on the way to some wider or different approach. Campbell Soup is a useful case in point. Only a year after creating its new North American Division, Campbell once again restructured its international operations. The company announced a new vision of "Campbell Brands Preferred Around the World," and the firm stated that it would now "look beyond just the Americas, across the Atlantic to Europe and across the Pacific to Asia."[222]

Why this change in approach? Part of the answer, we suspect, is that by this time it was no longer obvious, as it seemed to be a few years ago, that the global economy would be structured in the future by regional trading blocs. The movement toward deeper European integration and monetary union had run into worsening political and economic opposition, and the future of the European unification project was more and more in doubt. Japan's economy was wobbling badly, and few believed that a Japanese-led trading bloc in Asia would emerge in the near future. The 1997 failure of the U.S. Congress to provide President Clinton with fast track negotiating authority has further slowed the movement toward a FTAA, while the MERCOSUR customs union, the most developed subregional trade group in the Americas, is bracing for the impact of major fiscal policy adjustments on the part of its leading member, Brazil. In the past few years, it has not been the Triad (the United States, Japan, and Europe) but rather the "big emerging markets" (BEMs) that have captured the attention of economists, columnists, and business leaders. Fashion counts as much in corporate organization as in the garment industry, and the rush has been to explore elegant new global solutions rather than the now somewhat dowdy regional bloc approach.

There may also be a tendency in the United States to take "North America" for granted in strategic terms. Many firms no longer view Canada as a "foreign" country. For an increasing number, as in the automotive industry, Mexico is not very foreign either. U.S. companies set up operations in Canada or in Mexico because that was where markets existed and where money could be made. "We came to Canada," says the CEO of one of America's largest retail-securities brokerages, "because we believed the services we offer are universal. They're not American; they're not Canadian. We feel very much at home."[223] The notion of "North America" may have become so commonplace that companies are less conscious of specific arrangements in the region.

Uncertainty about Mexico is another dimension of the answer. Turning Mexico into an export platform appears to be an ideal strategy, but some firms see great difficulties in doing this if Mexico's domestic market fails to revive. "We cannot survive only by assembling things and exporting them," said the head of Ford Mexico. "We need a strong internal market and local revenues." Without the stimulation of an expanding domestic market, this executive felt that his company might consider shifting investment to Brazil, where demand is higher.[213] Moreover, substantial doubts remain with regard to Mexico's capacity to create the kind of modern infrastructure required to support world class production. The shift to "new" maquiladora production is heavily dependent on Mexico's capacity to create a supportive infrastructure.

Technological advance also keeps changing the parameters of corporate structure and strategy. As firms look out beyond the next few years, they see vast uncertainties about the impact of technological innovation. If downsized, out-sourced, even "virtual" companies are the wave of the future, the issue of where to site large new production facilities grows less and less relevant. If automation drastically reduces traditional blue-collar labor from most manufacturing operations, then the calculation of costs in final production changes radically, and low-cost labor no longer provides significant competitive advantage.

Our conclusions still stand, however. Outside of a major economic catastrophe, pressures on U.S. firms to integrate across North America will continue and even intensify. Many more approaches to and models of continental integration may emerge, but we can speak with confidence of a dynamic, rapidly evolving and deepening North American economy.

Endnotes

1. Nancy Dunne, Stephen Fidler, and Patti Waldmeir, 1997, "Old Wounds to Reopen," *The Financial Times*, June 30.

2. Economic Policy Institute, 1997, "NAFTA a Failure Thus Far, Group Reports, Should Be Repealed or Drastically Revised," press release in July on the publication of a report entitled *The Failed Experiment: NAFTA at Three Years.*

3. Quoted in "U.S. Jobless Point Finger at NAFTA," 1997, *Globe and Mail*, February 25.

4. Raymond Keating, 1997, "History's Hard Road," *Journal of Commerce*, September 30.

5. Quoted in Peter Morton, 1997, "U.S. Report Sings NAFTA's Praises," *The Financial Post*, July 12.

6. Paul Krugman and Robert Z. Lawrence, 1994, "Trade, Jobs and Wages," *Scientific American* (April).

7. *Study on the Operation and Effects of the North American Free Trade Agreement*, transmitted by the Executive Office of the President of the United States to Congress as required by section 512 of the NAFTA Implementation Act, July 1997, i-ii.

8. Sidney Weintraub, 1996, "Nafta Benefits Flow Back and Forth Across the Rio Grande," *The Wall Street Journal*, May 10.

9. See Stephen Blank, 1993, "The Emerging Architecture of North America," North-South Agenda Paper One, March (Coral Gables, Fla.: North-South Center, University of Miami).

10. Stephen Krajewski, 1992, *Multinational Firms Across the Canada-U.S. Border: An Investigation of Intrafirm Trade and Other Activities* (Ottawa: The Conference Board of Canada), April. Krajewski joined the research team at the Americas Society in 1993. Additional data derived from The Conference Board of Canada survey were published with The Conference Board's permission as Working Paper #2 in the Americas Society Series: Stephen Krajewski, 1993, *Adjusting to the New North American Competitive Dynamic: The Experience of U.S. Subsidiaries in Canada* (New York: Americas Society), January.

11. Stephen Blank, Stephen Krajewski, and Henry Yu. 1995. *U.S. Firms in North America: Redefining Structure and Strategy, North American Outlook* 5:2 (March) (Washington, D.C.: National Planning Association).

12. Scott Wallinger, Senior Vice President, International Operations, The Westvaco Corporation, interview by Stephen Krajewski, 1993.

13. See James Brian Quinn, Thomas Doorley, and Penny Pacquette, 1990, "Technology in Services: Rethinking Strategic Focus," *Sloan Management Review* (Winter).

14. Brent Jang, 1996, "Oil Patch Looks South," *The Globe and Mail*, December 9.

15. See John Fayerweather, 1973, *Foreign Investment in Canada: Prospects for National Policy* (White Plains, N.Y.: International Arts and Sciences Press, Inc.).

16. See Joseph LaPalombara and Stephen Blank, 1976, *Multinational Corporations and National Elites: A Study in Tensions: Conference Board Report No. 702* (New York: Conference Board); and Fayerweather 1973, 8-12. Opinion polls in the early 1960s showed that a majority of Canadians felt there was enough U.S. capital in Canada. By 1973, surveys showed that only one-third of all Canadians thought that American investment in Canada was a "good thing," while almost half felt it was "bad."

17. Kari Levitt, 1970, *Silent Surrender: The Multinational Corporation in Canada* (Toronto: Macmillan of Canada), 25.

18. Fayerweather 1973, 34; LaPalombara and Blank 1976, 26-27.

19 . The Foreign Investment Review Act (C.S. 1974, c. 46) and its operative arm, the Foreign Investment Review Agency, were recommended initially in the Gray Report. The Act came into effect in 1974. The operations of the Agency were expanded in October 1975.

20. LaPalombara and Blank 1976, 60.

21. J. Herbert Smith, 1976, "FIRA's Obligation: Understand Parent, Subsidiary Relations," *Financial Times of Canada*, May 3.

22. Maude Barlow, 1991, "The Free Trade Agreement Fails Canada," in *The Challenge of the Canada-United States Free Trade Agreement: An Assessment from Many Perspectives, The American Review of Canadian Studies,* eds. Marshall Cohen and Stephen Blank, Twentieth Anniversary special issue, Summer/Autumn.

23. Maxwell A. Cameron, Lorraire Eden, and Maureen Appel Molot, 1992, "North American Free Trade: Co-Operation and Conflict in Canada-Mexico Relations," in *Canada Among Nations 1992-1993: A New World Order?* eds. Fen Osler Hampson and Christopher Maule (Ottawa: Carlton University Press), 174.

24. Leonard Waverman, 1991, "A Canadian View of North American Economic Integration," in *Continental Accord: North American Economic Integration*, ed. Steven Globerman (Vancouver: Fraser Institute), 31.

25. Waverman 1991, 31.

26. Richard Lipsey, 1990, "Canada at the U.S.-Mexico Free Trade Dance: Wallflower or Partner," *Commentary*, No. 20; Ron Wonnacott, 1990, "U.S. Hub-and-Spoke Bilaterals and the Multilateral Trading System," *Commentary*, No. 20.

27. *Globe and Mail*, February 2, 1993.

28. Leonard Waverman, 1993, "The NAFTA Agreement: A Canadian Perspective" (Vancouver: The Fraser Institute), 50-56.

29. Cameron, et al., 1992, 185.

30. Nora Lustig, 1992, *Mexico: The Remaking of an Economy* (Washington, D.C.: The Brookings Institution), 125.

31. Roger D. Hansen, 1971, *The Politics of Mexican Development* (Baltimore: Johns Hopkins University Press), 15-77.

32. Whiting 1992, 59-60.

33. John Coatsworth, 1989, "The Decline of the Mexican Economy," in *América Latina en la época de Simón Bolívar*, ed. R. Liehr (Berlin: Colloquium Verlag).

34. Juan Carlos Moreno and Jaime Ros, 1994, "Market Reform and the Changing Role of the State in Mexico: A Historical Perspective," in *The State, Markets and Development*, eds. Amita Dutt, Kwan S. Kim, and Ajit Singh (London: Edward Elgar), 115.

35. Moreno and Ros 1994, 116.

36. Whiting 1992, 61.

37. Timothy King, 1970, *Mexico: Industrialization and Trade Policies since 1940* (New York: Oxford University Press), 10-11; Clark Reynolds, 1970, *The Mexican Economy: Twentieth Century Structure and Growth* (New Haven, Conn.: Yale University Press).

38. In 1982, the state owned approximately 1,155 enterprises, which accounted for 14 percent of GDP and 30 percent of gross fixed capital formation. By 1992, the government owned 286 of these enterprises, a drop of 80 percent. See Roderic Ai Camp, 1993, *Politics in Mexico* (New York: Oxford University Press), 167.

39. Barbara Jenkins, 1992, *The Paradox of Continental Production: National Investment Policies in North America.* Ithaca, N.Y.: Cornell University Press, 163.

40. Camp 1993, 166-199.

41. It is argued that the ISI began to backfire for many reasons: local manufacturing products began to saturate the consumer market; traditional commodity production and exports began to lag, creating growing balance-of-payments problems; and, finally, protectionism, or the high tariff barriers used to protect domestic manufacturing goods from competition by low cost imports, resulted in industrial inefficiency. All of these created the severe stagnation of the economy and triggered inflation. See Michael Twomey, 1993, *Multinational Corporations and the North American Free Trade Agreement* (Westport, Conn.: Praeger Publishers), 14-19.

42. Gray Newman and Anna Szterenfeld, 1993, *Business International's Guide to Doing Business in Mexico* (New York: McGraw-Hill, Inc.), 5.

43. The peso fell from 447 to the U.S. dollar in 1985 to 2,379 to the dollar by the end of 1987 (Jenkins 1992, 179).

44. Salinas targeted inflation as one of the main objectives of his administration and developed as an economic strategy the Pact of Stability and Economic Growth, whose goals included the reduction of the public deficit, holding prices constant, holding wages constant, and a further devaluation of the peso (Jenkins 1992, 70). The pact was a trilateral agreement among government, business, and labor leaders that started in 1987. The results were as follow: inflation dropped from 159.2 percent in 1987 to 51.7 percent in 1988. The 1991 inflation rate dropped to an unprecedented 18.8 percent, and in 1992 inflation decreased again to 11.9 percent (Newman and Szterenfeld 1993, 5).

45. These included 1) The investment must not exceed US$100 million; 2) financing of the project must be wholly external — investors already established in Mexico may use funds they already possess in Mexico; 3) the initial investment must be worth at least 20 percent of the total investment; 4) the investment must be made outside certain geographical zones where industrial activity is currently concentrated (including Mexico City, Monterrey, and Guadalajara); 5) the new entity must achieve a positive balance of payments during the first three years in operation; 6) the investment must generate new jobs and set up training programs; and 7) appropriate technology must be used, with attention to Mexico's environmental needs. Information taken from Government of Mexico, 1989, *Reglamento de la Ley para Promover la Inversión Mexicana y Regular la Inversión Extranjera* (Mexico City: Government of Mexico).

46. Lustig 1992. Prior to 1989, foreign investment laws, including the 1973 Technology Transfer Law and the 1976 Law of Inventions and Trademarks, were restrictive. There were activities: a) reserved for the state, b) reserved exclusively for Mexicans, c) limited to a certain percentage set below the maximum 49 percent, and (d) limited to a ceiling of 49 percent.

47. Pedro Aspe, 1993, *Economic Transformation: The Mexican Way* (Cambridge, Mass.: MIT Press).

48. Wilson Peres Núñez, 1990, *Foreign Direct Investment and Industrial Development in Mexico* (Paris: Organization for Economic Cooperation and Development, OECD).

49. This took place through adoption of the following measures: 1) a phaseout of import tariffs; 2) elimination or reduction of nontariff barriers, including import quotas, licenses, and technical barriers to trade; 3) establishment of clear, binding protection for intellectual property rights; 4) creation of fair and expeditious dispute-settlement procedures; and 5) creation of means to improve and expand the flow of goods, services, and investment between the two countries (Newman and Szterenfeld 1993, 12).

50. Newman and Szterenfeld 1993, 14.

51. Jenkins 1992, 178.

52. Acquisitions of existing firms resulting in more than 49 percent foreign ownership require approval from the Foreign Investment Commission, which is part of the Secretariat of Commerce and Industrial Development (Secofi). Some large mergers or acquisitions may be subject to review by the Federal Competition Commission under Mexico's antitrust law, which went into effect in June 1993. This law gives Mexico's anti-monopoly authorities, the Federal Competition Commission (CFC), more muscle to take on some of the country's biggest players. The CFC has a reputation for not doing much about monopolies in the past, but it has quietly begun to tackle practices like price-fixing and cartels. It has had a hand in bringing competition to such areas as petroleum, credit-card and laundry services, and telecommunications.

53. Regarding restrictions on land ownership, the Agrarian Law of 1992 allows corporate ownership of agricultural land, but there are still restrictions that apply. Foreign companies are free to acquire non-agricultural land.

54. In addition, Mexico has a number of free ports where imports can be stored with no tax levied until the importer markets them. There are also several free zones, although officials are working out plans to phase out these zones and eliminate their duty-free status.

55. Patricia Wilson, 1992, *Exports and Local Development* (Austin, Texas: University of Texas Press), 37.

56. Newman and Szterenfeld 1993, 214.

57. Wilson 1992, 40.

58. During the first stage (1965-1982), maquiladoras were primarily just a regional development program. They employed mostly young single female workers with low educational backgrounds. In 1972, President Luis Echevarría Alvarez (1970-1976) changed the name of the program to Mexican Industrialization Program (MIP), permitting the implementation of maquiladoras in any part of Mexico except heavily industrialized areas such as Monterrey, Guadalajara, and Mexico City. Labor demands and an overvalued peso diminished the competitive nature of the Mexican maquiladoras next to those in Asia or the Caribbean. Finally, the U.S. recession of 1973-1974 caused a drop in employment, and the

Mexican government reacted. President José López Portillo (1976-1982) devalued the peso in 1976 and created the Alliance for Production, which cut most of the red tape implemented in the 1971 regulations for establishing maquiladoras (Wilson 1992, 40).

59. Wilson 1992, 40.

60. Newman and Szterenfeld 1993, 217.

61. Wilson 1992, 41

62. Wilson 1992, 42-45.

63. It should be noted that, in spite of growing competition in international markets, the Mexican maquiladora industry still provided employment for about 20 percent of the Mexican labor force in 1995. This highlights the importance of globalized integrated markets for Mexican workers.

64. Wilson 1992, 46.

65. Tim Coone, 1995, "Mexico: On the Borderline," *Business Latin America*, December 18, 6.

66. Edward Y. George, 1990, "What Does the Future Hold for the Maquiladora Industry?" in *The Maquiladora Industry: Economic Solution or Problem?* ed. Khosrow Fatemi (New York: Praeger).

67. Khosrow Fatemi, ed., 1990, *The Maquiladora Industry: Economic Solution or Problem?* (New York: Praeger Publishers); Coone 1995, 6.

68. Kevin G. Hall, 1995, "Mexico Exports Soar with Devaluation of Peso," *Journal of Commerce*, June 27.

69. Newman and Szterenfeld 1993, 157.

70. In the years between 1962 and 1983, regulations on the automotive industry increased in periods of recession and decreased in periods of growth. However, the sector was incapable of reducing its foreign trade deficit, which reached $2.3 billion between the years of 1978 and 1981 (Newman and Szterenfeld 1993, 160). Among the regulations required can be cited 1) 60 percent of the parts/components contained in vehicles put together in Mexico had to be sourced locally (measured in direct cost terms); 2) all finished motors and other critical parts, such as transmissions, shock absorbers, and drive shafts, were required to be produced in Mexico (they could not be imported); 3) all completely knocked-down or semi-knocked-down kits from which cars were manufactured (normally containing a maximum of 20 percent local content) were prohibited from being imported, as were fully assembled vehicles; and 4) government price controls and production quotas were established (Newman and Szterenfeld 1993, 157-159).

71. María de Lourdes Guzmán, 1997, *Automotive Original Equipment Manufacturer's Market* (Mexico City: U.S. and Foreign Commercial Service, U.S. Department of Commerce), 2.

72. Newman and Szterenfeld 1993, 162-163.

73. Newman and Szterenfeld 1993, 162-163.

74. Furthermore, calculation of local content would no longer be tied to cost-of-parts or materials imports, but would instead be defined on the basis of national value added, determined by subtracting imports from the total domestic and foreign sales. In addition, four important provisions were set to protect the prior investors in the sector. The total number of

vehicles imported into Mexico could not exceed 15 percent of domestic sales (Mexican) during the 1991 and 1992 model years for each manufacturer. The figure would be raised to 20 percent for 1993 and 1994 model years. Second, for every U.S. dollar value of new cars imported, the manufacturer would export two (US) dollars and fifty cents ($2.50) for the 1991 model year, $2.00 for the 1992 and 1993 model years, and $1.75 for the 1994 model year. Third, overall, vehicle manufacturers would have to maintain a positive trade balance to be permitted the above import privileges. Finally, at least 36 percent of a vehicle's content would have to be sourced domestically from the Mexican autoparts industry, down from the previous 50-60 percent local content requirement (Newman and Szterenfeld 1993, 166-167).

75. IDC-select, 1997, *Tendencias 1997* (Mexico: IDC).

76. Newman and Szterenfeld 1993, 198.

77. Newman and Szterenfeld 1993, 200.

78. Newman and Szterenfeld 1993, 201.

79. MNCs operating under the former decrees may import up to 80 percent of the value added to their Mexican production and investments in manufacturing facilities (stock) duty free. These same companies may import up to 200 percent of their investments in technology, including software development programs, also duty free (Newman and Szterenfeld 1993, 202).

80. Jenkins 1992, 182-183.

81. The privatization took place in two stages. In the first stage, begun in 1990, the Bank Disincorporation Committee received itemized operation strategies from prospective bidders, explaining how they proposed to operate the bank. The committee decided which bidder qualified. The second stage, consisting of the sale itself, was carrried out on a price basis and to bidders who qualified during the first phase.

82. Newman and Szterenfeld 1993, 242-247.

83. Newman and Szterenfeld 1993, 247.

84. Newman and Szterenfeld 1993, 248.

85. Citibank has been the only foreign bank operating in Mexico since 1930 that was not affected by nationalization but has had limited retail exposure (Gray Newman, 1994, "Crossing the Mexican Banking Border," *Business Latin America*, May 16, 1).

86. Thomas Legler, 1995, *A Comparison of Canadian and Mexican Postwar Development (1945-1994)* (Mexico City: Centro de Investigaciones Sobre América del Norte, Universidad Nacional Autónoma de México), 31.

87. Joseph D'Cruz and James Fleck, 1988, *Yankee Canadians in the Global Economy: Strategic Management of U.S. Subsidiaries Under Free Trade* (London, Ontario: The National Centre for Management Research and Development, The University of Western Ontario), 9. See also Isaiah Litvak, 1990, "U.S. Multinationals: Repositioning the Canadian Subsidiary," *Business in the Contemporary World* (Autumn).

88. CPC International, 1991, *Annual Report 1990* (Englewood Cliffs, N.J.: CPC International).

89. See D'Cruz and Fleck, 1998, Chapter 7.

90. Gilles Rheaume and Jacek Warda, 1994, *The Role of Foreign-Owned Subsidiaries in Canada* (Ottawa: The Conference Board of Canada).

91. Interview with Pablo Rosales, General Director, Honeywell, Mexico; North-South Center survey 1994-1996.

92. Newman and Szterenfeld 1993, 37.

93. Newman and Szterenfeld 1993, 37.

94. Interview with Garen Chu, Regional Controller, Singer Mexicana, Mexico City; North-South Center survey 1994-1996.

95. Amy Barrett, 1991, "Hail to the Chef," *Financial World*, June 11, 52-53.

96. Zeffrey Zygmont, 1993, "In Command at Campbell," *Sky Magazine* (March), 60.

97. Bill Saporito, 1991, "Campbell Soup Gets Piping Hot," *Fortune* (September), 143.

98. Whirlpool Corporation, 1989, *Annual Report for 1988* (Benton Harbor, Mich.: Whirlpool Corporation); Whirlpool Corporation, 1990, *Annual Report for 1989* (Benton Harbor, Mich.: Whirlpool Corporation).

99. William Marohn, Executive Vice President, North American Appliance Group, quoted in Anne Henry, 1991, "The Consolidation Story," *Appliance* (June), W-83.

100. See Isaiah Litvak, 1990, "U.S. Multinationals: Repositioning the Canadian Subsidiary," *Business in the Contemporary World* (Autumn); and D'Cruz and Fleck, 1988, Chapter 1.

101. To build durable associations with overseas partners, consistency in quality and efficient service will be critical. This is precisely where many Mexican firms fall short. Concepts of total quality and the adoption of international standards are still very new in Mexico. Total quality systems focus on the human behavior and organizational factors in production processes involving everybody from the telephone operator to the managing director. However, little progress has been made in Mexico, the reason in most cases being lack of management commitment. The maquiladora sector is the most advanced in adopting total quality programs because of its integration into international manufacturing systems. However, as mentioned before, since these plants are poorly integrated into the domestic Mexican manufacturing sector, their effect on the overall economy has been insignificant (Coone 1995, 2-3).

102. Interview with David Lustig, by Stephen Krajewski, December 1993.

103. Interview with David Lustig, 1993.

104. North-South Center survey 1994-1996 of U.S. subsidiaries in Mexico.

105. E. Nef, 1985, *Canada-U.S. Free Trade: U.S. Perspective and Approaches*. Study prepared for the Ontario Ministry of Industry, Trade and Technology, quoted in D'Cruz and Fleck 1988.

106. Stephen Krajewski 1993, 6.

107. Robert Reich, 1991, *The Work of Nations* (New York: Vintage Books), 89.

108. Interview with Jaime White from Xerox Mexicana; North-South Center Survey 1994-1996.

109. Greg Ip, 1995, "Free Canada," *The Financial Post 500 1995* (Toronto: The Financial Post).

110. Campbell Soup Company, 1991, *Annual Report, 1990* (Camden, N.J.: Campbell Soup Company, 3.

111. Steven Krajewski 1993, 6.

112. Frank Popoff, 1992, *Dow Today*, No. 138, December 4.

113. Quoted in Margaret Studer, 1993, "ABB to Reorganize Its Global Structure into Three Regions," *Wall Street Journal*, August 25.

114. Quoted in Stephen Krajewski 1993, 6.

115. William Etherington, President, IBM Canada, quoted in Carolyn Leitch, 1992, "IBM Building North American Bloc," *The Globe and Mail*, May 7, B1.

116. J.P. Cousin, Vice President, Americas Operations, Xerox Company, interview by Stephen Krajewski, November 1993.

117. E.S. Browning, 1993, "Nafta or Not, Many Foreign Companies View North America as One Market," *Wall Street Journal*, November 15.

118. Denis Wilcock, quoted in *Dow Today*, No. 89, July 8, 1992.

119. Wilcock 1992, 89.

120. Sergio Sarmiento, 1997, "Mexico's Inevitable Transformation," *The Washington Quarterly* 20:4 (Autumn), 129.

121. Robert Chodos, Rae Murphy, and Eric Hamovitch, 1993, *Canada and the Global Economy* (Toronto: James Lorimer & Company), 132.

122. Krajewski 1992.

123. Krajewski 1992.

124. American Chamber of Commerce of Mexico, 1994, *NAFTA Goes to Work; A Survey of Companies Operating in Mexico: Preliminary Results of NAFTA Implementation* (Mexico City: American Chamber of Commerce of Mexico, A.C.), April.

125. Krajewski 1993, 12.

126. Interview with Garen Chu, North-South Center survey 1994-1996.

127. William Neuman and Mimi Cauley de la Sierra, 1994, *Responding to Change in Mexico* (New York: The Economist Intelligence Unit), 108-110.

128. Neuman and Cauley de la Sierra 1994, 93.

129. Robert W. Haigh, 1992, "Building a Strategic Alliance: The Hermosillo Experience as a Ford-Mazda Proving Ground," *The Columbia Journal of World Business* (Spring): 61-64, 73.

130. Rheaume and Warda, 1994.

131. Gordon Wilson, partner with Dingle & Wilson, Inc., quoted in John Southerst, 1993, "The Incredible Shrinking CEO," *Canadian Business*, October.

132. Stephen Krajewski 1993.

133. Stephen Krajewski and Stephen Blank, in cooperation with IBM, researched and prepared the information in this section.

134. John Akers, 1992, *Annual Report 1991* (Armonk, N.Y.: IBM), 2, 6.

135. Akers 1992, 4.

136. Quote from *The Globe and Mail*, June 30, 1993, B-23.

137. Interview with José María González, Black and Decker, North-South Center survey 1994-1996.

138. *Dow Today* 140, December 7, 1997.

139. Interview by Steven Krajewski, October 1992.

140. Ian Lennox, CEO of Monsanto Canada, quoted in Southerst 1993.

141. David Nattress, Vice President, Monsanto Canada, quoted in M. Daniel Rosen, 1990, "Monsanto Canada & The Brass Tacks of Global Business," *Monsanto Magazine,* November 4, 9.

142. Barry Burton, et al., 1993, "Restructuring in Canadian Subsidiaries of American Multinational Corporations," a confidential paper prepared for the Americas Society, May.

143. Geoffrey Rowan, 1996, "Canadian Managers Turn U.S. Heads," *The Globe and Mail,* June 12.

144. See Bernard Simon, 1995, "Minority Shareholders Play Hard to Get," *Financial Times*, July 18; "Vanishing Minority Shareholders," 1995, *The Globe and Mail*, February 15; and Gord MaLaughlin, 1995, "Canadian Stockholders Caught in Parental Vice," *The Financial Post*, July 22-23.

145. Newman and Szterenfeld 1993, 50-52.

146. Allen J. Morrison and Kendall Roth, 1993, "Developing Global Subsidiary Mandates," *Business Quarterly* (Summer), 105.

147. Krajewski 1993, 7.

148. Peter Rankine, Vice President and General Manager, Residential and Building Controls Group, Honeywell Corporation, n.d., quoted in Honeywell Limited (Canada), *Direction for the 90's* (Minneapolis: Honeywell Limited), 5.

149. David Lyle of Fisher Controls, quoted in Daniel Rosen, 1990, "Monsanto Canada and the Brass Tacks of Global Business," *Monsanto Magazine*, November 4.

150. Morrison and Roth 1993, 104.

151. Krajewski 1993, 6.

152. Krajewski 1993, 6.

153. Krajewski 1993, 10.

154. Krajewski 1993, 5-6.

155. Christopher Lorenz, 1991, "Hard Times for Country Cousins," *Financial Times*, December 13.

156. Quoted in John Southerst 1993.

157. Government of Canada, Department of Foreign Affairs and International Trade, 1995, "Lightolier Canada; Taking Advantage of a Niche Strategy to Win a North American Mandate," *Attracting World Mandate; Perspectives from Canadian CEOs* (Ottawa: Government of Canada).

158. Government of Canada, Department of Foreign Affairs and International Trade, 1995, "Hughes Aircraft of Canada Limited, How a Canadian Subsidiary Remains Viable in a Changing Economy," *Attracting World Mandate; Perspectives from Canadian CEOs* (Ottawa: Government of Canada).

159. Ip 1995, "Free Canada."

160. Interview with José María González.

161. Interview with Guillermo Ruiz Aguilar, Vice President, Kodak Mexicana; North-South Center survey 1994-1996

162. Greg Ip, 1995, "Fighting for Investment in the Era of Free Trade," *The Financial Post*, June 17.

163. Gerardo Otero, 1996, "Mexico's Economic and Political Futures," in *Neoliberalism Revisited: Economic Restructuring and Mexico's Political Future* (Westport, Conn.: Westview Press).

164. For an alternative viewpoint, Enrique Dussel Peters argues that import liberalization, the overvalued exchange rate, high real interest rates, and domestic divestment generated disincentives for manufacturing; yet this sector has been the most successful in attracting FDI and increasing productivity. Enrique Dussel Peters, 1996, "Changes in Mexico's Manufacturing Sector," in *Neoliberalism Revisited: Economic Restructuring and Mexico's Political Future*, ed. Gerardo Otero (Westport, Conn.: Westview Press).

165. Guillermo Ortiz, cited in "Mexico's Economy Regains Some Gusto," 1997, *The Globe and Mail*, October 9.

166. Sidney Weintraub, 1997, testimony before the Subcommittee on Trade, U.S. House of Representatives, Washington, D.C., September 11.

167. Aaron Tornell and Gerardo Esquivel, 1995, *The Political Economy of Mexico's Entry into NAFTA*, National Bureau of Economic Research, Working Paper 5322 (October).

168. Craig Torres, 1997, "Foreigners Snap Up Mexican Companies," *The Wall Street Journal*, Sepember 30.

169. Whiting 1992.

170. Torres 1997.

171. David A. Dean, 1995, "The Road to Recovery in Mexico," *The Journal of Commerce*, September 7.

172. Kevin G. Hall, 1995, "Mexican Exports Soar with Devaluation of Peso," *The Journal of Commerce,* June 27.

173. R. Sean Randolph, 1995, "Mexican Trade: A Look Ahead," *Journal of Commerce*, June 7.

174. James Sterngold, 1996, "NAFTA Trade-Off: Some Jobs Lost, Others Gained," *The New York Times*, October 7.

175. Nancy Dunne and Daniel Combey, 1997, "Peso Crisis Turbocharges Revolution in Motor Trade," *Financial Times*, June 11.

176. Allen R. Myerson, 1995, "Out of Crisis and Opportunity," *The New York Times*, September 25.

177. Myerson 1995.

178 . Geri Smith, Stanley Reed, and Elisabeth Malkin, 1995, "Mexico: A Rough Road Back," *Business Week*, November 13, 104-107.

179 . Gerri Smith and Stanley Reed, 1995, "Survival Strategies from Mexico's Front Lines," *Business Week*, November 13.

180. Kevin G. Hall 1995.

181. "Industry Brief Retail," 1997, *Business Latin America*, August 4.

182. "Industry Brief Retail" 1997.

183. Elisabeth Malkin, 1995, "Pitching to Peso-Pinchers," *Business Week*, May 15.

184. Mark Stevenson, 1996, "Mexico: Strategies for Survival," *Business Latin America*, January 29.

185. Stevenson 1996.

186. Stevenson 1996.

187. "Marketing Watch," 1997, *Business Latin America*, October 20, 7.

188. "Marketing Watch" 1997.

189. Mark Stevenson, 1997, "On a Roll," *Business Latin America*, August 4, 3.

190. Sidney Weintraub, 1997a, *NAFTA at Three: A Progress Report* (Washington, D.C.: Center for Strategic and International Studies), 10.

191. Report issued by Red Mexicana de Acción sobre Libre Comercio (RMALC), 1997, *NAFTA: At the Center of the Crisis* (Mexico City: RMALC).

192. Cited in "Mexico's Economy Regains Some Gusto," *The Globe and Mail*, October 9, 1997.

193. Rafael Fernández de Castro, 1997, testimony before the Subcommittee on the Western Hemisphere, U.S. House of Representatives, Washington, D.C., September 17.

194. Maude Barlow and Bruce Campbell, 1991, *Take Back the Nation* (Toronto: Key Porter Books, Ltd.), 9.

195. Barlow and Campbell 1991, 9-10.

196. Barlow and Campbell 1991, 11-12.

197. J.L. Granatstein, 1996, *Yankee Go Home: Canadians and Anti-Americanism* (Toronto: Harper Collins Canada), 276-277.

198. Nancy Dunne, 1997, "Canada Takes Free Trade Trail Alone," *Financial Times*, April 11.

199. See Conrad Winn, 1997, "FP/COMPASS Poll; Post 2000," *Financial Post*, October 4.

200. Quoted in Granatstein 1996, 277.

201. Gordon Ritchie, 1997, "Sitting on Top of the World," *Financial Post*, October 4.

202. Rebecca Goldfarb, 1997, "Canadian Broadcasting Policy: The Struggle to Preserve a Distinct Identity," in *Canadian Cultures and Globalization* 19, Canadian Issues and Themes, Association of Canadian Studies, eds. Joy Cohenstaedt and Yves Frenette.

203. This is not to suggest, however, that restructuring is not particularly painful in Canada. The lack of adjustment in Canadian manufacturing industries in the mid-1980s was responsible for a sharp divergence in U.S. and Canadian productivity growth in this period. "This inferior productivity performance, combined with a further deterioration in relative

wages and the near-30 percent appreciation of the dollar (from trough to peak) generated a colossal unit-labour-cost disparity" with the United States. Thomas Courchene, 1992, "Mon pays, c'est l'hiver: Reflections of a Market Populist," *Canadian Journal of Economics*, November, 76.

204. John Southerst, 1992, "There Goes the Future," *Canadian Business*, October.

205. Rod McQueen, 1996, "The New Canadian Establishment," *Financial Post*, February 17.

206. Executive Office of the President of the United States 1997, i.

207. Sidney Weintraub 1997a, 22.

208. Andrew Cohen, 1997, "World-Weary U.S. Looking Inward," *The Globe and Mail*, September 22.

209. Rafael Fernández de Castro, 1997, testimony before the Subcommittee on the Western Hemisphere, U.S. House of Representatives, Washington, D.C., September 14.

210. William Diebold, 1984, "Canada and the United States: Twenty-five Years of Economic Relations," *International Journal* 39:2 (Spring), 404.

211. Julian Birkinshaw and Warren Ritchie, 1993, "Balancing the Global Portfolio," *Business Quarterly* (Summer).

212. Birkinshaw and Ritchie 1993.

213. Blank 1993.

214. Southerst 1993.

215. See "The Border," 1997, *Business Week*, May 12.

216. For a useful discussion of such solutions, see Julian Birkinshaw, 1995, "Encouraging Entrepreneurial Activity in Multinational Corporations," *Business Horizons* 38:3 (May).

217. James Brian Quinn, Thomas Doorley, and Penny Paquette, 1990, "Beyond Products: Services-Based Strategy," *Harvard Business Review* (March-April).

218 . Charles Handy, 1994, "Tender, Loving Care for Better Workers," *Financial Times*, February 21.

219. Birkinshaw 1995.

220. Charles Handy, 1992, "Balancing Corporate Power: A New Federalist Paper," *Harvard Business Review* (November-December), 61.

221. Quoted in "The Very Model of Efficiency," 1992, *The New York Times*, March 2.

222. Campbell Soup Company, 1992, *Annual Report 1991* (Camden, N.J.: Campbell Soup Company); Campbell Soup Company, 1994, *Annual Report 1993* (Camden, N.J.: Campbell Soup Company).

223. Stanley Reed and Elisabeth Malkin, 1995, "Survival Strategies from Mexico's Front Lines," *Business Week,* November 13.

References

Akers, John. 1992. *Annual Report 1991.* Armonk, N.Y.: IBM.

American Chamber of Commerce of Mexico. 1994. *NAFTA Goes to Work. A Survey of Companies Operating in Mexico: Preliminary Results of NAFTA Implementation.* Mexico City: American Chamber of Commerce of Mexico.

Aspe, Pedro. 1993. *Economic Transformation: The Mexican Way.* Cambridge, Mass.: MIT Press.

Barlow, Maude. 1991. "The Free Trade Agreement Fails Canada." In *The Challenge of the Canada-United States Free Trade Agreement: An Assessment from Many Perspectives,* eds. Marshall Cohen and Stephen Blank. Twentieth anniversary special issue of *The American Review of Canadian Studies* (Summer/Autumn).

Barlow, Maude, and Bruce Campbell. 1991. *Take Back the Nation.* Toronto: Key Porter Books, Ltd.

Barrett, Amy. 1991. "Hail to the Chef." *Financial World,* June 11.

Bartlett, Christopher A., and Sumanthra Ghoshal. 1989. *Managing Across Borders.* Boston: Harvard Business School Press.

Birkinshaw, Julian. 1995. "Encouraging Entrepreneurial Activity in Multinational Corporations." *Business Horizons* 38:3 (May).

Birkinshaw, Julian, and Warren Ritchie. 1993. "Balancing the Global Portfolio." *Business Quarterly* (Summer).

Blank, Stephen. 1993. "The Emerging Architecture of North America." North-South Center Agenda Paper One (March). Coral Gables, Fla.: North-South Center Press.

Blank, Stephen, Stephen Krajewski, and Henry Yu. 1995. *U.S. Firms in North America: Redefining Structure and Strategy, North American Outlook* 5:2 (March). Washington, D.C.: National Planning Association.

Browning, E.S. 1993. "Nafta or Not, Many Foreign Companies View North America as One Market." *Wall Street Journal,* November 15.

Burton, Barry, et al. 1993. "Restructuring in Canadian Subsidiaries of American Multinational Corporations," confidential paper presented to the Americas Society, May.

Business Latin America. 1975. "Mexico's New Investment Regs Herald Closer Scrutiny of Foreign Company Practices." December 17.

Business Latin America. 1975. "Official Mexican Study Criticizes Foreign Investment." April 30.

Business Latin America. 1997. "Industry Brief Retail." August 4.

Business Latin America. 1997. "Marketing Watch." October 20.

Business Week. 1997. "The Border." May 12.

Cameron, Maxwell A., Lorrair Eden, and Maureen Appel Molot. 1992. "North American Free Trade: Co-Operation and Conflict in Canada-Mexico Relations." In *Canada Among Nations 1992-1993: A New World Order?* eds. Fen Osler Hampson and Christopher Maule. Ottawa: Carlton University Press.

Camp, Roderic Ai. 1993. *Politics in Mexico.* 1st ed. New York: Oxford University Press.

Camp, Roderic Ai. 1996. *Politics in Mexico*. 2nd ed. New York: Oxford University Press.

Campbell Soup Company. 1991. *Annual Report 1990*. Camden, N.J.: Campbell Soup Company.

Campbell Soup Company. 1992. *Annual Report 1991*. Camden, N.J.: Campbell Soup Company.

Campbell Soup Company. 1994. *Annual Report 1993*. Camden, N.J.: Campbell Soup Company.

Centeno, Miguel Angel. 1994. *Democracy Within Reason: Technocratic Revolution in Mexico*. University Park, Pa.: Pennsylvania State University Press.

Chodos, Robert, Ray Murphy, and Eric Hamovitch. 1993. *Canada and the Global Economy*. Toronto: James Lorimer & Company.

Chu, Garen. Interview. North-South Center Survey 1994-1996.

Clark, Kim B., and Steven C. Wheelwright. 1993. *Managing New Product and Process Development: Text and Cases*. New York: The Free Press.

Coatsworth, John. 1989. "The Decline of the Mexican Economy, 1800-1860." In *América Latina en la época de Simón Bolívar*, ed. R. Liehr. Berlin: Colloquium Verlag.

Cohen, Andrew. 1997. "World-Weary U.S. Looking Inward." *The Globe and Mail*, September 22.

Coone, Tim. 1995. "Mexico: On the Borderline." *Business Latin America*, December 18.

Cothran, Dan A. 1994. *Political Stability and Democracy in Mexico: The "Perfect Dictatorship."* Westport, Conn.: Praeger Publishers.

Courchene, Thomas. 1992. "Mon pays, c'est l'hiver: Reflections of a Market Populist." *Canadian Journal of Economics* (November).

Cousin, J.P. 1993. Interview by Stephen Krajewski. November.

CPC International. 1991. *Annual Report 1990*. Englewood Cliffs, N.J.: CPC International.

D'Cruz, Joseph, and James Fleck. 1998. *Yankee Canadians in the Global Economy: Strategic Management of U.S. Subsidiaries under Free Trade*. London, Ontario: The National Centre for Management Research and Development, The University of Western Ontario.

Dean, David A. 1995. "The Road to Recovery in Mexico," *Journal of Commerce*. September 7.

Del Castillo, Gustavo. 1996. "NAFTA and the Struggle for Neoliberalism: Mexico's Elusive Quest for First World Status." In Gerardo Otero, ed. *Neoliberalism Revisited: Economic Restructuring and Mexico's Political Future*. Boulder, Colo.: Westview Press.

Diebold, William. 1984. "Canada and the United States: Twenty-five Years of Economic Relations." *International Journal* 39:2.

Dow Chemical Corporation. 1993. *Annual Report 1992*. Midland, Mich.: Dow Chemical Corporation.

Dow Today. July 8, 1992.

Dow Today. December 4, 1997. 138.

Dow Today. December 7, 1997. 140.

Drucker, Peter F. 1992. *Managing for the Future*. New York: Dutton.

Dunne, Nancy. 1997. "Canada Takes Free Trade Trail Alone." *The Financial Times*, April 11.

Dunne, Nancy, and Daniel Combey. 1997. "Peso Crisis Turbocharges Revolution in Motor Trade." *The Financial Times*, June 11.

Dunne, Nancy, Stephen Fidler, and Patti Waldmeir. 1997. "Old Wounds to Reopen." *The Financial Times*, June 30.

Dussel Peters, Enrique. 1996. "Changes in Mexico's Manufacturing Sector." In *Neoliberalism Revisited: Economic Restructuring and Mexico's Political Future*, ed. Gerardo Otero. Boulder, Colo.: Westview Press.

Economic Policy Institute. 1997. "NAFTA a Failure Thus Far, Group Reports Should Be Repealed or Drastically Revised." Press release on the publication of a report entitled *The Failed Experiment: NAFTA at Three Years*. July.

Executive Office of the President of the United States. 1997. *Study on the Operation and Effects of the North American Free Trade Agreement*. Washington, D.C.: Office of the President of the United States. July.

Fatemi, Khosrow, ed. 1990. *The Maquiladora Industry: Economic Solution or Problem?* New York: Praeger Publishers.

Fayerweather, John. 1973. *Foreign Investment in Canada: Prospects for National Policy.* White Plains, N.Y.: International Arts and Science Press, Inc.

Fernández de Castro, Rafael. 1997. Testimony before the Subcommittee on the Western Hemisphere, U.S. House of Representatives, Washington, D.C. September 14.

Fernández de Castro, Rafael. 1997. Testimony before the Subcommittee on the Western Hemisphere, U.S. House of Representatives, Washington, D.C. September 17.

George, Edward Y. 1990. "What Does the Future Hold for the Maquiladora Industry?" In *The Maquiladora Industry: Economic Solution or Problem?* ed. Koshrow Fatemi. New York: Praeger Publishers.

Globe and Mail, The. 1993, February 2.

Globe and Mail, The. 1993, June 30.

Globe and Mail, The. 1995. "Vanishing Minority Shareholders," February 15.

Globe and Mail, The. 1997. "U.S. Jobless Point Finger at NAFTA," February 25.

Globe and Mail, The. 1997. "Mexico's Economy Regains Some Gusto," October 9.

Goldfarb, Rebecca. 1997. "Canadian Broadcasting Policy: The Struggle to Preserve a Distinct Identity." In *Canadian Cultures and Globalization* 19, Canadian Issues and Theme, Association of Canadian Studies, eds. Joy Cohenstaedt and Yves Frenette.

González, José María. Interview, North-South Center Survey 1994-1996.

Government of Canada, Department of Foreign Affairs and International Trade. 1995. "Hughes Aircraft of Canada Limited, How a Canadian Subsidiary Remains Viable in a Changing Economy." *Attracting World Mandate; Perspectives from Canadian CEOs*. Ottawa: Government of Canada.

Government of Canada, Department of Foreign Affairs and International Trade. 1995. "Lightolier Canada; Taking Advantage of Niche Strategy to Win a North American Mandate." *Attracting World Mandate; Perspectives from Canadian CEOs*. Ottawa: Government of Canada.

Government of Mexico. 1989. *Reglamento de la Ley para Promover la Inversión Mexicana y Regular la Inversión Extranjera*. Mexico City: Government of Mexico.

Granatstein, J.L. 1996. *Yankee Go Home: Canadians and Anti-Americanism*. Toronto: Harper Collins Canada.

Grosse, Robert E. 1989. *Multinationals in Latin America*. London: Routledge.

Grosse, Robert E., and Jack N. Behrman. 1990. *International Business and Governments: Issues and Institutions*. Columbia, S.C.: University of South Carolina Press.

Guzmán, María de Lourdes. 1997. *Automotive Original Equipment Manufacturer's Market.* Mexico City: U.S. Foreign Commercial Service, U.S. Department of Commerce.

Haigh, Robert W. 1992. "Building a Strategic Alliance: The Hermosillo Experience as a Ford-Mazda Proving Ground." *The Columbia Journal of World Business* (Spring): 6-173.

Hall, Kevin G. 1995. "Mexican Exports Soar With Devaluation of Peso," *Journal of Commerce*, June 27.

Hamel, Gary, and C.K. Prahalad. 1994. *Competing for the Future.* Boston: Harvard Business School Press.

Hammer, Michael, and James Champy. 1993. *Reengineering the Corporation: A Manifesto for Business Revolution.* New York: Harper Business.

Handy, Charles. 1992. "Balancing Corporate Power: A New Federalist Paper." *Harvard Business Review* (November-December).

Handy, Charles. 1994. "Tender, Loving Care for Better Workers." *Financial Times*, February 21.

Hansen, Roger D. 1971. *The Politics of Mexican Development.* Baltimore: Johns Hopkins University Press.

Henry, Anne. 1991. "The Consolidation Story." *Appliance* (June).

Heskett, James L., W. Earl Sasser, Jr., and Christopher W.L. Hart. 1990. *Service Breakthroughs.* New York: The Free Press.

Honeywell Limited (Canada). n.d. *Direction for the '90s.* Minneapolis: Honeywell Limited.

IDC-Select. 1997. *Tendencias 1997.* Mexico: International Data Corporation (IDC).

Ip, Greg. 1995. "Fighting for Investment in the Era of Free Trade." *The Financial Post*, June 17.

Ip, Greg. 1995. "Free Canada." In *The Financial Post 500 1995.* Toronto: The Financial Post.

Jang, Brent. 1996. "Oil Patch Looks South." *The Globe and Mail,* December 9.

Jenkins, Barbara. 1992. *The Paradox of Continental Production: National Investment Policies in North America.* Ithaca, N.Y.: Cornell University Press.

Journal of Commerce. 1996. "Maquiladora Growth Strong." June 25.

Keating, Raymond. 1997. "History's Hard Road." *Journal of Commerce.* September 30.

King, Timothy. 1970. *Mexico: Industrialization and Trade Policies Since 1940.* New York: Oxford University Press.

Krajewski, Stephen. 1992. *Multinational Firms Across the Canada-U.S. Border: An Investigation of Intrafirm Trade and Other Activities.* Ottawa: The Conference Board of Canada. April.

Krajewski, Stephen. 1993. *Adjusting to the New North American Competitive Dynamic: The Experience of U.S. Subsidiaries in Canada.* Americas Society Working Paper #2, January. New York: Americas Society.

Krugman, Paul, and Robert Z. Lawrence. 1994. "Trade, Jobs and Wages." *Scientific American* (April).

LaPalombara, Joseph, and Stephen Blank. 1976. *Multinational Corporations and National Elites: A Study in Tensions. Conference Board Report No. 702.* New York: Conference Board.

Legler, Thomas. 1995. *A Comparison of Canadian and Mexican Postwar Development (1945-1994).* Mexico City: Centro de Investigaciones sobre América del Norte, Universidad Nacional Autónoma de México.

Leitch, Carolyn. 1992. "IBM Building North American Bloc." *The Globe and Mail*, May 7.

Levitt, Keri. 1970. *Silent Surrender: The Multinational Corporation in Canada*. Toronto: Macmillan of Canada.

Lipsey, Richard. 1990. "Canada at the U.S.-Mexico Free Trade Dance: Wallflower or Partner." *Commentary* (No. 20).

Litvak, Isaiah. 1990. "U.S. Multinationals: Repositioning the Canadian Subsidiary." *Business in the Contemporary World* (Autumn).

Lorentz, Christopher. 1991. "Hard Times for Country Cousins." *Financial Times*, December 13.

Luke, Paul. 1988. "Debt and Oil-Led Development: The Economy Under López Portillo (1977-1982)." In *The Mexican Economy*, ed. George D.E. Philip. London: Routledge.

Luna, Matilda. 1995. "Entrepreneurial Instincts and Political Action in Mexico: Facing the Demands of Economic Modernization." In *The Challenge of Institutional Reform in Mexico*, ed. Riordan Roett. Boulder, Colo.: Lynne Rienner Publishers.

Lustig, David. Interview by Stephen Krajewsky, December 1993.

Lustig, Nora. 1992. *Mexico: The Remaking of an Economy*. Washington, D.C.: The Brookings Institution.

MaLaughlin, Gord. 1995. "Canadian Stockholders Caught in Parental Vice." *The Financial Post*, July 22-23.

Malkin, Elizabeth. 1995. "Pitching to Peso-Pinchers: Mexico's Slump Has Forced U.S. Marketers to Be Creative." *Business Week*, May 15.

McQueen, Rod. 1996. "The New Canadian Establishment." *Financial Post*, February 17.

Moreno, Juan Carlos, and Jaime Ros. 1994. "Market Reform and the Changing Role of the State in Mexico: A Historical Perspective." In *The State, Markets and Development*, eds. Dutt Amitava, Kwan S. Kim, and Ajit Singh. London: Edward Elgar.

Morrison, Allen J., and Kendall Roth. 1993. "Developing Global Subsidiary Mandates." *Business Quarterly* (Summer).

Morton, Peter. 1997. "U.S. Report Sings NAFTA's Praises." *The Financial Post*, July 12.

Myerson, Allen R. 1995. "Out of Crisis and Opportunity." *The New York Times*, September 25.

Neuman, William, and Mimi Cauley de la Sierra. 1994. *Responding to Change in Mexico*. New York: The Economist Intelligence Unit.

Newman, Gray. 1994. "Crossing the Mexican Banking Border," *Business Latin America*. May 16.

Newman, Gray, and Anna Szterenfeld. 1993. *Business International's Guide to Doing Business in Mexico*. New York: McGraw-Hill, Inc.

New York Times, The. 1992. "The Very Model of Efficiency," March 2.

Ohmae, Kenichi. 1985. *Triad Power*. New York: The Free Press.

Otero, Gerardo, ed. 1996. *Neoliberalism Revisited: Economic Restructuring and Mexico's Political Future*. Boulder, Colo.: Westview Press.

Otero, Gerardo. 1996. "Mexico's Economic and Political Futures." In *Neoliberalism Revisited: Economic Restructuring and Mexico's Political Future*, ed. Gerardo Otero. Boulder, Colo.: Westview Press.

Peters, Enrique Dussel. 1996. "Changes in Mexico's Manufacturing Sector." In *Neoliberalism Revisited: Economic Restructuring and Mexico's Political Future*, ed. Gerardo Otero. Boulder, Colo.: Westview Press.

Peres Nuñez, Wilson. 1990. *Foreign Direct Investment and Industrial Development in Mexico*. Paris: Organization of Economic Cooperation and Development (OECD).

Philip, George D. E., ed. 1998. *The Mexican Economy*. London: Routledge.

Porter, Michael E. 1985. *Competitive Advantage*. New York: The Free Press.

Quinn, James Brian, Thomas Doorley, and Penny Paquette. 1990. "Beyond Products: Services-Based Strategy." *Harvard Business Review* (March-April).

Quinn, James Brian, Thomas Doorley, and Penny Paquette. 1990. "Technology in Services: Rethinking Strategic Focus." *Sloan Management Review* (Winter).

Quinn, James Brian. 1992. *Intelligent Enterprise: A Knowledge and Service Based Paradigm for Industry*. New York: The Free Press.

Randall, Laura, ed. 1966, *Changing Structure of Mexico: Political, Social, and Economic Prospects*. Columbia University Seminar Series. Armonk, N.Y.: M. E. Sharpe.

Randolph, R. Sean. 1995. "Mexican Trade: A Look Ahead," *The Journal of Commerce*. June 7.

Rankine, Peter. n.d. Cited in *Direction for the 90's*. Minneapolis: Honeywell, Limited.

Red Mexicana de Acción sobre Libre Comercio (RMALC). 1997. *NAFTA: At the Center of the Crisis*. Mexico City: RMALC.

Reed, Stanley, and Elisabeth Malkin. 1995. "Survival Strategies from Mexico's Front Lines." *Business Week*. November 13.

Reich, Robert. 1991. *The Work of Nations*. New York: Vintage Books.

Reynolds, Clark W. 1970. *The Mexican Economy: Twentieth Century Structure and Growth*. New Haven: Yale University Press.

Rheaume, Gilles, and Jacek Warda. 1994. *The Role of Foreign-Owned Subsidiaries in Canada*. Ottawa: The Conference Board of Canada.

Ritchie, Gordon. 1997. "Sitting on Top of the World." *Financial Post*, October 4.

Rosales, Pablo. Interview. North-South Center Survey 1994-1996.

Rosen, M. Daniel. 1990. "Monsanto Canada & The Brass Tacks of Global Business." *Montsanto Magazine*. November 4.

Rowan, Geoffrey. 1996. "Canadian Managers Turn U.S. Heads." *The Globe and Mail*, June 12.

Ruiz Aguilar, Guillermo. Interview, North-South Center Survey 1994-1996.

Sachs, Jeffrey, Aaron Tornell, and Andrés Velasco. 1995. *The Collapse of the Mexican Peso: What Have We Learned?* Working Paper 5142. Cambridge, Mass.: National Bureau of Economic Research.

Sarmiento, Sergio. 1997. "Mexico's Inevitable Transformation." *The Washington Quarterly* 20:4.

Saporito, Bill. 1991. "Campbell Soup Gets Piping Hot." *Fortune* (September).

Simon, Bernard. 1995. "Minority Shareholders Play Hard to Get." *Financial Times*, July 18.

Smith, J. Herbert. 1976. "FIRA's Obligation: Understand Parent, Subsidiary Relations." *Financial Times of Canada,* May 3.

Smith, Gerri, and Stanley Reed. 1995. "Survival Strategies from Mexico's Front Lines." *Business Week*. November 13.

Smith, Gerri, Stanley Reed, and Elisabeth Malkin. 1995. "Mexico: A Rough Road Back." *Business Week*. November 13.

Southerst, John. 1992. "There Goes the Future." *Canadian Business* (October).

Southerst, John. 1993. "The Incredible Shrinking CEO." *Canadian Business* (October).

Sterngold, James. 1996. "NAFTA Trade-Off: Some Jobs Lost, Others Gained." *The New York Times*, October 7.

Stevenson, Mark. 1996. "Mexico: Strategies for Survival." *Business Latin America*. January 29.

Stevenson, Mark. 1997. "On a Roll." *Business Latin America*. August 4.

Story, Dale. 1986. *Industry, the State and Public Policy in Mexico*. Austin: University of Texas.

Studer, Margaret. 1993. "ABB to Reorganize Its Global Structure into Three Regions." *The Wall Street Journal*, August 25.

Tornell, Aaron, and Gerardo Esquivel. 1995. *The Political Economy of Mexico's Entry into NAFTA*. Working Paper 5322. Cambridge, Mass.: National Bureau of Economic Research.

Torres, Craig. 1997. "Foreigners Snap Up Mexican Companies." *The Wall Street Journal*, September 30.

Twomey, Michael J. 1993. *Multinational Corporations and the North American Free Trade Agreement*. Westport, Conn.: Praeger Publishers.

Valdés Ugalde, Francisco. 1994. "From Bank Nationalization to State Reform: Business and the New Mexican Order." In *The Politics of Economic Restructuring*, eds. Maria Loren Cook, Kevin J. Middlebrook, and Juan Molinar Horcasitas. La Jolla, Calif.: Center for Mexican Studies, University of California, San Diego.

Wallinger, Scott. Interview by Stephen Krajewski. 1993.

Waverman, Leonard. 1991. "A Canadian View of North American Economic Integration." In *Continental Accord: North American Economic Integration,* ed. Steven Globerman. Vancouver: Fraser Institute.

Waverman, Leonard. 1993. *The NAFTA Agreement: A Canadian Perspective*. Vancouver: The Fraser Institute.

Weintraub, Sidney. 1996. "Nafta Benefits Flow Back and Forth Across the Rio Grande." *The Wall Street Journal*, May 10.

Weintraub, Sidney. 1997a. *NAFTA at Three: A Progress Report*. Washington, D.C.: Center for Strategic and International Studies.

Weintraub, Sidney. 1997b. Testimony before the Subcommittee on Trade, U.S. House of Representatives, Washington, D.C., September 11.

White, Jaime. Interview, North-South Center Survey 1994-1996.

Whiting, Van. 1992. *The Political Economy of Foreign Direct Investment in Mexico*. Baltimore: Johns Hopkins University Press.

Wilson, Patricia A. 1992. *Exports and Local Development*. Austin, Texas: University of Texas Press.

Whirlpool Corporation. 1989. *Annual Report for 1988*. Benton Harbor, Mich.: Whirlpool Corporation.

Whirlpool Corporation. 1990. *Annual Report for 1989*. Benton Harbor, Mich.: Whirlpool Corporation.

Winn, Conrad. 1997. "Sitting on Top of the World." *Financial Post*, October 4.

Wonnacott, Ron. 1990. "U.S. Hub-and-Spoke Bilaterals and the Multilateral Trade System." *Commentary*, No. 23.

Zygmont, Zeffrey. 1993. "In Command at Campbell." *Sky Magazine* (March).

Appendix

Companies Participating in the Americas Society Study and the North-South Center Survey

Allied Signal
American Cyanamid Company
Ameritech
Bell Helicopter Textron, Inc.
Black and Decker
Bridgestone/Firestone
Campbell Soup Company
Continental Airlines
CPC International, Inc.
Dana Corporation
Del Monte
Direc Spicer
Dow Chemical Company
Dupont
Duracell
Eastman Kodak Company
Eli Lilly
Exxon
FMC Corporation (Ford)
Foote, Cone and Belding
Freeport-McMoran, Inc.
General Electric Company
Goodman Equipment Corporation
GTE
Hoechst-Celanese Corporation
Honeywell, Inc.
IBM
Kone Elevators America

Kroll Associates
Levi Strauss
Mead
Mobil
Monsanto
Motorola, Inc.
NCR
Pepsi-Cola International
Pfizer International
Revlon
Rockwell Int'l. Overseas Corp.
Schering-Plough International
Singer
Texas Instruments
The Procter & Gamble Co.
The Gillette Company
Unilever United States, Inc.
United Airlines
W.R. Grace & Company
Warner-Lambert
Westvaco
Whirlpool Corporation
Wyeth Ayerst Int'l., Inc.
Xerox Corporation

Index

A

Aeroméxico, 12
Akers, John, 52
alliances, strategic, 48-49
Argentina, 14
Asea Brown Boveri Ltd., 42
auto industry: Mexican market for autos,
    17;
    Mexico, 17-18, 66-67
Automotive Decree (1989), Mexico, 17
autonomy: of Canadian managers in U.S.
    firms in Canada, 7, 21;
    changes for U.S. Canadian operations
        in (1988-94), 49-52;
    changes for U.S. Mexican operations in
        (1988-95), 52-54;
    in response to North American
        integration, 54-55;
    U.S. subsidiaries in Canada and Mexico,
        49

B

banking system, Mexico, 11-12, 19
Barlow, Maude, 71
Barnevik, Percy, 42
Barshefsky, Charlene, ix
Birkinshaw, Julian, 77
Black & Decker: Canada, 41, 60;
    distribution in Mexico, 47;
    Mexico, 54, 60-61
Bolivia, 71
Border Industrialization Program (BIP),
    Mexico, 15
Brazil, 14
Bush, George, 8

C

Campbell, Bruce, 71
Campbell Soup Company, 28-29, 41, 83
Canada: competitive advantage of, 59-60,
    63;

development policy (late 1800s), 5-6;
effect of oil price shocks (1973, 1979,
    1982), 7-8;
hearings related to proposed NAFTA
    negotiations, 8-9;
increased exports of, 63;
perception of foreign direct investment,
    5-8;
perception of U.S. investment in, 6;
pre-NAFTA perception of Mexico, 8-10;
resistance to trade liberalization and
    economic integration, 73;
U.S. exports to (1993-96), ix;
view of foreign direct investment in,
    5
Canada-U.S. Free Trade Agreement
    (CUSFTA), x;
    Canadian adjustment to, 37-38;
    Canadian criticism of, 8, 37, 80;
    negotiations and conclusion (1989), 8;
    opportunities provided by, 57, 59
capital flows, Mexico, 11
Chile: Mexican free trade agreement with,
    14;
    opposition to extension of NAFTA, 75;
    proposed extension of NAFTA to, ix
Chrétien, Jean, 72
Chrétien, Raymond, 4
Chrysler México, 17, 66-67
Coca-Cola, 68
Cohen, Andrew, 75
Colgate-Palmolive, 69
Colombia, 71
Commission for Environmental Coopera-
    tion (CEC) (NAFTA), 75
Commission for Labor Cooperation (CLC)
    (NAFTA), 75
companies *See firms.*
competition: among U.S. subsidiaries in
    Canada and Mexico, 56-61;